Angel Threads

Lark Books
50 College Street
Asheville, North Carolina

10 9 8 7 6 5 4 3 2 1

Library of Congress Catalog Card Number: 86-81517

ISBN 0-937274-20-8

Printed in Hong Kong by South China Printing Company

Angel Threads

Creating Lovable Clothes for Little Ones

Text and Illustrations by
Karen Ericsson Martin

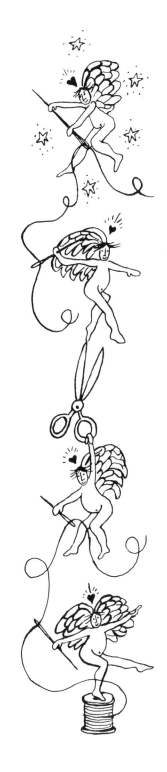

Lark Books
Asheville, North Carolina

FOR MY THREE FAVORITE ANGELS

CONTENTS

~ GUARDIAN ANGEL ~

POEM:

The sky is full of stardust,
It will be lighter soon;
An Angel with a little cloud
Is dusting off the moon.
~ A.F. Brown

INSTRUCTIONS FOR MAKING THE GUARDIAN ANGEL ARE ON PAGE 99.

INTRODUCTION

Hundreds of years ago, textiles were itemized not far behind precious metals as the most valuable personal belongings in household inventories. Nearly all clothing was worn as long as possible, repaired, remodeled, or dyed a different color and then passed to the next generation, where the whole process probably began again. Even when a family was considered well-to-do, fabric was rarely thrown away. The clothing was often given away, but not until the precious laces, buttons, and trimmings of all kinds were carefully removed for another use. Threads and yarns of very worn woven and knitted fabrics enjoyed a reserved space in the scrap bag until time could be found to unravel them and wind them into balls to be used again.

Children's clothing was usually made from reusable portions of older siblings' or adults' worn-out garments or parts of old household linens. The Winterthur Museum in Delaware once displayed an infant's dress embellished with polychromed crewel flower motifs which was, according to textile experts, probably made from a used bed curtain! The cunning sleeves of the gown came from another, unidentified, piece of linen.

As recently as fifty years ago, if fabrics chosen for a baby's clothing weren't perceived to be especially beautiful, family seamstresses put their own personal mark on styles adapted from the old country with fancy stitches and special applied decorations. The results were true labors of love. The infant apparel was usually made well enough to be handed down to many generations of children, as was the clothing of American Colonial times. Wearable examples with a tattered beauty still turn up today in antique and thrift shops as immortal reminders of their makers. These thrift shop finds and the philosophy that handmade is very special are the inspiration for this book.

The projects featured here can help you create some unique first-year outfits and accessories. The patterns are easy to follow, easy to assemble, and will adapt readily to different uses, depending upon your fabrics. The choices illustrated in the book are only suggestions, for it is hoped that you will use your imagination to come up with your own fabric, yarn, and color combinations. In the "use it up, wear it out" approach of our ancestors, fabrics you have right at home can kindle the flame of your imagination at a cost of next to nothing. We urge you to look in a different way at old or new embroidered handkerchieves, dresser scarves, napkins, a favorite old blouse, skirt, dress, pants, old blankets, dishtowels, socks, bandanas, scarves, and even new dishcloths. The source of inspiration from out-of-the-ordinary fabrics is not limited to your home—second-hand clothing shops and dime stores are fertile ground for the makings of surprisingly beautiful baby clothes. Remember as you look for pretty snippets of unusual textiles that covering a baby takes a very small amount of fabric. The softness of a many-times-washed fabric next to a baby's tender skin, the thought of all those known and unknown ancestors who wore and enjoyed life in that piece of cloth ages ago, and the special value and enjoyment of making something by hand by yourself, are all comforting concepts in today's fast-paced computerized world.

Though it takes little fabric to sew for an angel and it needn't cost much to create something heavenly, the fancy stitches and special decorations you choose to add to your creations will take time and effort. The results of any extra work you do, however, will surely make the final product that much more charming, deserving of you, your baby, future generations—and the name angel threads.

1

SOURCES

Look around you for wonderful cast-offs. You may be one of those fortunate people who has been given beautiful textiles by your relatives for some auspicious occasion such as a wedding. Or just because you are the person they know will appreciate the hours of work the items represent. If your family heirlooms went to the Salvation Army long ago, go there now and look for replacements. It's a treasure hunt! You will find that thrift shopping soon becomes a passion not easily dissuaded. The person who enjoys working with textiles is passing up a wonderful source of exceptional handwork if she doesn't explore these outlets.

Most communities have at least one such store. Besides the "Sally," other philanthropical groups such as St. Vincent de Paul's, the Rescue Mission, associations for retarded citizens, Junior Leagues, service leagues, to name only a few, run shops which sell second-hand merchandise. Look in your yellow pages under "Thrift Shops" for a complete listing in your area.

Many of the things you will be looking for are too much bother for people today as they need special care (e.g. ironing). Don't be fooled into thinking they will be purchased for pennies, but prices will be reasonable. You are sure to find old linens and some laces well within your budget, but there are an increasing number of collectors and dealers out there competing for the merchandise. You can feel pleased about the good use you will be making of your purchases, and the good causes to which you are contributing. Soon, however, you might find yourself unable to pass up any beautiful little snippets, and collecting or hoarding in spite of yourself. Beware!

Keep your eyes open for:

— used packages of trims, ribbons

— old and new laces or slips, blouses, and linens trimmed with special ones that you can remove

— old linens of all kinds—tablecloths, napkins, dresser scarves, hand towels, tea towels, handkerchieves

— embroidered work that can be cut from used clothing

— yarns and flosses—for embroidery, braiding, tassels, pom-poms, edgings, mock tatting, knitting, crocheting

— ball and tassel fringes—the balls and tassels can be cut from the trim and used separately; the braid can be used as an edging on jackets, robes, vests, coats

— buttons—any flat button, especially the common "pearl" shirt button, is an often-overlooked decorative device, especially when applied to the back of a baby's clothing. The back is seen so much by other people during the first months and there is no chance of baby's little fingers grabbing buttons sewn on the back.

The wonderful new novelty buttons now available to the consumer often can be the focal point of a baby ensemble! Collect a large variety. On a vest or sweater, a row of several different buttons is charming. Or the applique motif you are using can often be repeated in the buttons. Any good sewing or craft store should have a wide selection from which to choose.

If you want a really special piece of linen or lace, an antique shop just might be your best shopping bet. Even at an antique shop price, you certainly couldn't duplicate the piece without a monumental effort of time, exquisite needlework skills, and patience. And at the prices of such new merchandise today, the antique price seems low by comparison. Do consider this option for that special-occasion outfit.

FABRICS AND FIBERS

Comfort is of primary importance for a baby's clothes. Fabrics and yarns should, above all, be soft. Although natural fiber fabrics are often thought of as best, and many older fabrics were only of cotton, linen, or wool fibers, some linens and woolens obviously would be too scratchy for a baby's tender skin unless lined with a softer fabric. This is a solution to keep in mind if you find an exquisite textile which has questionable "hand." Always use your own good common sense when choosing textiles for re-use.

Care is another important factor. If the garment to be made is for special occasions, it is not crucial that it be easy to care for, as it won't be laundered or cleaned as often as a more casual, everyday garment. One of the benefits of incorporating old textile treasures into your own angel threads is the many times they have probably been washed. Many women saved their loveliest linens for an event that never came. Others had the attitude that some things were just too beautiful to use and packed them away for what turned out to be almost forever.

Fabrics should always be washed before you begin to sew, but if you are quite sure you will be using an heirloom that has never been laundered, it is even more important to analyze its washability. Gentle is the by-word for washing old fabrics and laces. A chlorine-free bluing will bring out any whiteness if the fabric has yellowed from age, but remember that many older linens were naturally off-white, ecru, or yellowish.

Spots, stains, and small tears or other such imperfections should not deter you from using a textile piece if the damage doesn't cover too large an area. Appliques, patches, and embroidery were used in the old days to hide and cover such problems. They add wonderful interest, texture, color, and beauty. Even mistakes often turn into ingenious approaches in your garment-making. In the past, many new needlework techniques were discovered as the result of error, so don't let perfectionism hinder your creativity! The results of embellishing over an error you have found or made might turn a pretty garment into one that's exceptionally beautiful.

3

COLOR AND TEXTURE

When was the last time you looked through a geographic or travel magazine? These often show plump-cheeked babies from other parts of the world in their native dress or national costume. How often do you see them dressed in pastel pink, blue, yellow, turquoise, and lavender? You are much more likely to see them wearing dark hues accented with bright primary colors and of a variety of textures. People in other countries tend to be more practical; soiling is rarely as noticeable on dark colors as on light.

We encourage you to expand your perceptions of how a baby should be dressed and of what looks best against a baby's skin. Black, dark browns, blues, greens and purples can enhance all of the possible skin tones more beautifully than you can imagine! Combinations of prints, plaids, checks, stripes work unbelievably well for baby clothing if the motifs are small scale.

Most instruction books tell you to buy enough fabric, or enough yarn of the same weight and dye lot, to complete a project. We advise you, instead, to be flexible and versatile, and to experiment with combinations of the above. A practice tension swatch for knitting will tell you how to adjust your needle size and yarn combinations to get the correct gauge for different yarn weights. Work up a sampler for fun. Cast on some stitches with number 7 needles, say. Work a few rows with one weight of yarn, then tie on a different weight and see what you have to do to compensate for the difference. Smaller needles or larger ones? Or should you be using, perhaps, two strands of that yarn? Work as many combinations as you have needles and yarn weights and you will soon see what you have to do to utilize all of the scraps of yarn you may have lying around.

5

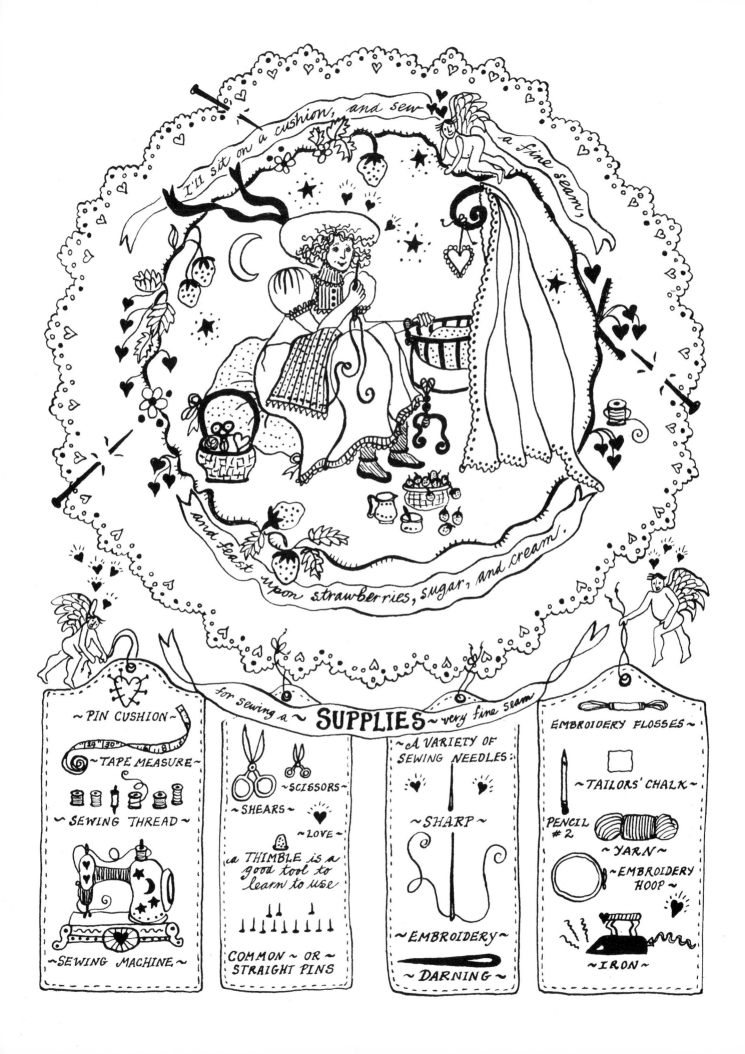

I'll sit on a cushion, and sew a fine seam,

and feast upon strawberries, sugar, and cream.

for sewing a ~ SUPPLIES ~ very fine seam

~ PIN CUSHION ~

~ TAPE MEASURE ~

~ SEWING THREAD ~

~ SEWING MACHINE ~

~ SCISSORS ~

~ SHEARS ~

~ LOVE ~

a THIMBLE is a good tool to learn to use

COMMON ~ OR ~ STRAIGHT PINS

~ A VARIETY OF SEWING NEEDLES ~

~ SHARP ~

~ EMBROIDERY ~

~ DARNING ~

EMBROIDERY FLOSSES ~

~ TAILORS' CHALK ~

PENCIL #2

~ YARN ~

~ EMBROIDERY HOOP ~

~ IRON ~

THE PATTERNS

Most of the patterns in this book are adaptations from our collection of old and antique children's clothing. Those from the 1920's and '30's are most desirable because the roomy fit and simple lines work so well for an heirloom look and offer so many possibilities for variations. They also are ample enough to accommodate today's slightly larger children. Baby clothes from earlier times look like today's doll clothes!

The goal of this book is to allow the experienced sewer to experiment with the wide variety of looks that can be obtained by using only a few simple patterns. We want you to learn to place fabrics on top of the pattern at times, rather than the pattern on top of the fabric as is the usual approach, so you will get an idea how parts of other articles of clothing can be used for a baby garment. For example: adult sleeves become baby pant legs!

The first Basic Pattern lets you design all kinds of gowns, robes, buntings, dresses, shirts, coats, jackets, and vests. It includes a petticoat pattern which can be used as a sundress or jumper, and a hood or bonnet pattern which takes on a new look with a change of fabric or fiber. The illustrations will help you to see the spectrum of design possibilities at your imagination's beck and call.

The second Basic Pattern is for jumpsuits, pants, and overalls. You won't believe how versatile you can be with this one when you open your eyes to the materials you have at hand that can be used in very unexpected ways. Riddle: When is a sweater not a sweater? Answer: When it is a pair of pants! You'll soon see what an easy answer that is.

Following the Basic Patterns are chapters on sweaters, footwear, bibs, ideas for decorating new, purchased clothing and for renovating used clothing to make it very special, and a series of nursery items and toys. Every one of the projects uses out-of-the-ordinary fabric sources to achieve exceptional additions to your baby's layette.

ABBREVIATIONS

Throughout the book we have used abbreviations in the project instructions. Most of them will be familiar to you, and they all should be self-explanatory.

Sewing terms:

B · back

F · front

C · center

CF · center front

CB · center back

SA · seam allowance

RST · right sides together

WST · wrong sides together

Knitting and crochet terms:

CO · cast on

K · knit

P · purl

SC · single crochet

DC · double crochet

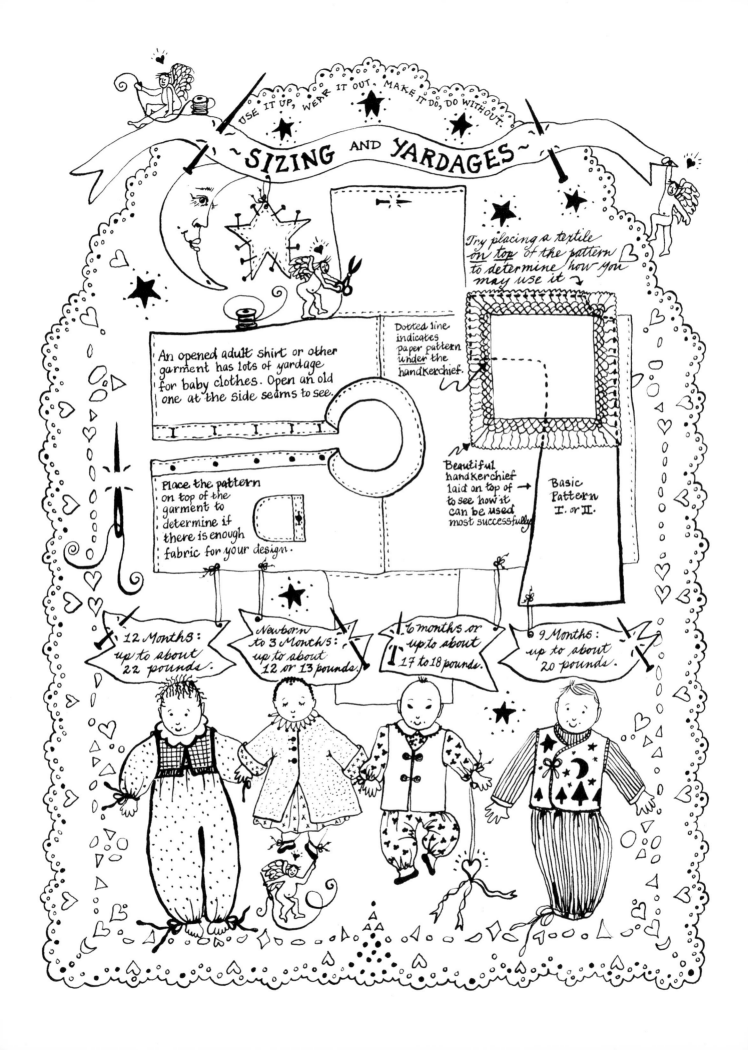

USE IT UP, WEAR IT OUT, MAKE IT DO, DO WITHOUT.

~SIZING AND YARDAGES~

Try placing a textile on top of the pattern to determine how you may use it →

An opened adult shirt or other garment has lots of yardage for baby clothes. Open an old one at the side seams to see.

Dotted line indicates paper pattern under the handkerchief.

Place the pattern on top of the garment to determine if there is enough fabric for your design.

Beautiful handkerchief laid on top of to see how it can be used most successfully

Basic Pattern I. or II.

12 Months: up to about 22 pounds.

Newborn to 3 Months: up to about 12 or 13 pounds.

6 months or up to about 17 to 18 pounds.

9 Months: up to about 20 pounds.

SIZING

If you have recently spent time looking at manufactured infant clothing because of the advent of a little angel in your life, you may be very confused when it comes time to make a decision regarding size. Contributing to your confusion are the discrepancies in size charts for specific age groups among many brand-name manufacturers. Not only does a newborn vary from "preemie" weight to 10 pounds or more, but the baby's length also affects the fit of his clothing.

For the most part, you should pay attention to the baby's size, or weight, not the age in months. In ready-made clothing, an infant usually will wear a garment size approximately six months larger than his actual age. Most size charts are based on the 50th percentiles (average) from regularly-scheduled growth and development studies. Pediatricians and other child-study/service professionals receive these charts on a regular basis. From them, general guidelines such as the one below are gleaned for the clothing industry:

Newborn to 3 months	— up to approximately 12 or 13 pounds
6 months	— up to approximately 17 or 18 pounds
9 months	— up to approximately 20 pounds
12 months	— up to approximately 22 pounds

The wisest decision the sewer and designer of infant clothing can make is to check the following pattern measurements against the baby's measurements. Then plan on "a little too big," as babies have a habit of growing a whole size in the wink of an eye!

Do not be concerned if the pattern dimensions in this book seem a little large to you. So many of today's baby clothes are constructed of knit fabrics which stretch over baby's body that they look tiny on the hanger but then expand amazingly on the human form. The patterns included here are designed to be used primarily with woven fabrics, so they must have much roomier dimensions.

The patterns included here are so simple that you can easily add or subtract a quarter of an inch along all straight lines. The hemlines in particular are only suggested lengths; you may want no hem (for a lace edging finely zigzagged to the raw fabric edge), or a hem of three inches for lots of growing room. As with all approaches in the book, the choice is yours.

YARDAGES:

This may be silly, because you are an experienced sewer if you are using this book, but do you have the following memorized for quick reference when you see something special?

4-1/2 inches = 1/8 yard
9 inches = 1/4 yard
12 inches = 1/3 yard
18 inches = 1/2 yard
27 inches = 3/4 yard
31-1/2 inches = 7/8 yard
36 inches = 1 yard

Do you carry a cloth tape measure with you when you are thrift shopping?

Basic Pattern I: GOWN AND FRIENDS

Most newborns spend much of their lives snuggled into comfortable cotton knit sacques. The basic Gown Pattern can, of course, be used to execute this ubiquitous staple of a baby's wardrobe, but as the new mother and father probably receive (or purchase at very reasonable prices) a good supply of sacques, the seamstress would be wise to spend her sewing time more creatively. Many of the ideas which follow are designed so that they can be worn over the comfortable knit gowns, thus expanding the baby's wardrobes for both winter and summer.

The basic Gown Pattern offers a multitude of wardrobe possibilities for a baby. All of the following garments can be made from it: gowns, robes, shirts, jumpers, vests, jackets, coats, dresses, sundresses, buntings. The pattern is cut large and of the utmost simplicity to encourage the seamstress to experiment with a wide range of combinations.

Look over one of the patterns to see the options you have. Add to them the Oriental-looking center front flap opening illustrated in the vest and tabard pattern, and you have even more! You will notice that there are three approximate-size patterns. They are all designed to be very roomy, so remember to check your pattern choice against the baby's measurements.

Depending upon your placement of the pattern against a lengthwise fold or a lengthwise raw edge of fabric, you will have a front or back neck opening. Any number of sleeve or hem lengths are available; the patterns have lines to signify where you can cut, but you may wish to cut at a different length, depending upon whim, the fabric you have chosen (the use of old clothing will affect your choice), and/or your baby's measurements.

On the newborn-to-three-months pattern page are also a side gusset, which accents the home-from-the-hospital gown, a bonnet or hood pattern with bonnet crown (please note that you must add ¼" all around the bonnet pattern for the two larger sizes of three-to-six-months and six-to-twelve-months), and a heart pattern to use as an applique. You may wish to cut larger or smaller hearts or use more or fewer in your designs. Experiment to see what pleases your eye!

Notice the cut-off lines for shirt, jacket, and vest, for dresses and coats, for day or night gowns, and for long robes and the christening gown. They are also to be taken as approximate. Measure your baby, allow for growth, and consider the hem before cutting. The dotted lines indicate cutting lines for the christening gown petticoat (which works nicely as a jumper and a sundress, too!), a sleeveless length, and a suggested cutting line for a newborn-size bunting.

-DRAWSTRING GOWN-

-SUNDRESS-

-DRESS WITH CORNER HANDKERCHIEVES DECORATED-

The Basic Gown has many FRIENDS for you to play with:

-Robes-
-Shirts-
-Dresses-
-Sundresses-
-Jumpers-
-Buntings-
-Vests-
-Coats-
-Jackets-

-VEST WITH SLEEVES FROM YOUR SWEATER-

-SHIRT WITH DETACHABLE SKIRT-

-BUNTINGS-

-ZIPPERED JUMPER-

-ROBE OR LONG DRESS-

Basic Pattern I
GOWN and FRIENDS

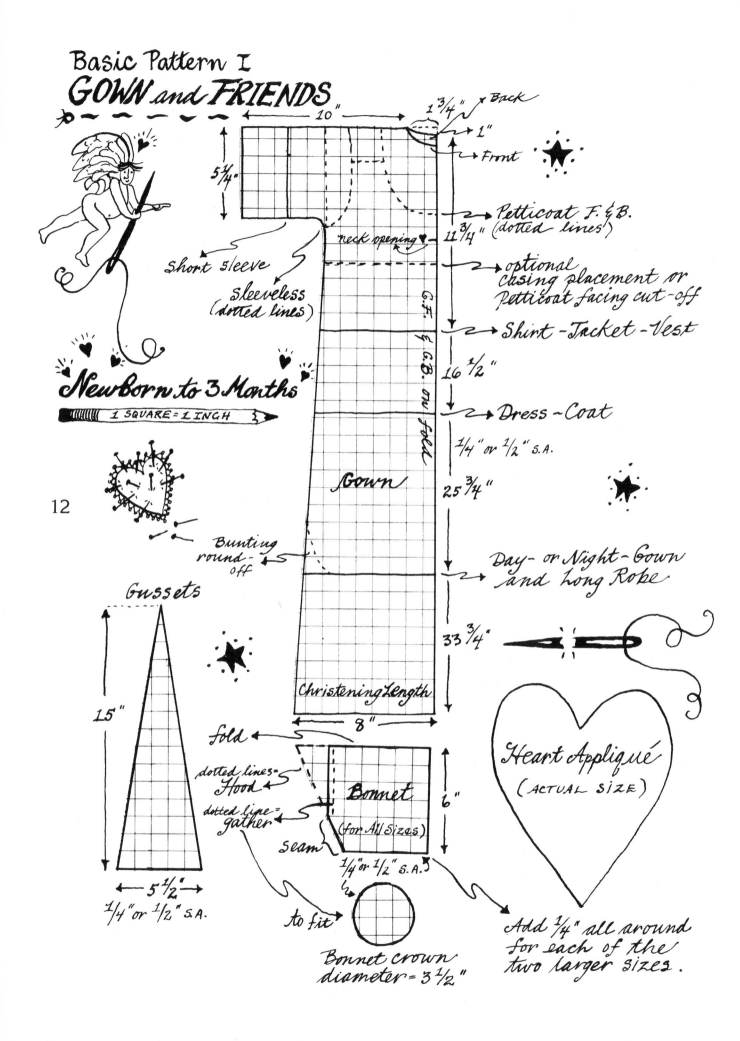

10"

5¾"

1¾" → Back

1" → Front

Petticoat F. & B.
(dotted lines)

11¾"

neck opening

optional casing placement or Petticoat facing cut-off

Short sleeve

sleeveless (dotted lines)

Shirt - Jacket - Vest

C.F. & C.B. on fold

16½"

Dress - Coat

¼" or ½" S.A.

Newborn to 3 Months

1 SQUARE = 1 INCH

Gown

25¾"

Day- or Night-Gown and Long Robe

12

Bunting round-off

Gussets

33¾"

15"

Christening Length

8"

5½"

¼" or ½" S.A.

fold

dotted lines = Hood

dotted line = gather

Bonnet
(for All Sizes)

6"

seam

¼" or ½" S.A.

to fit

Bonnet crown diameter = 3½"

Heart Appliqué
(ACTUAL SIZE)

Add ¼" all around for each of the two larger sizes.

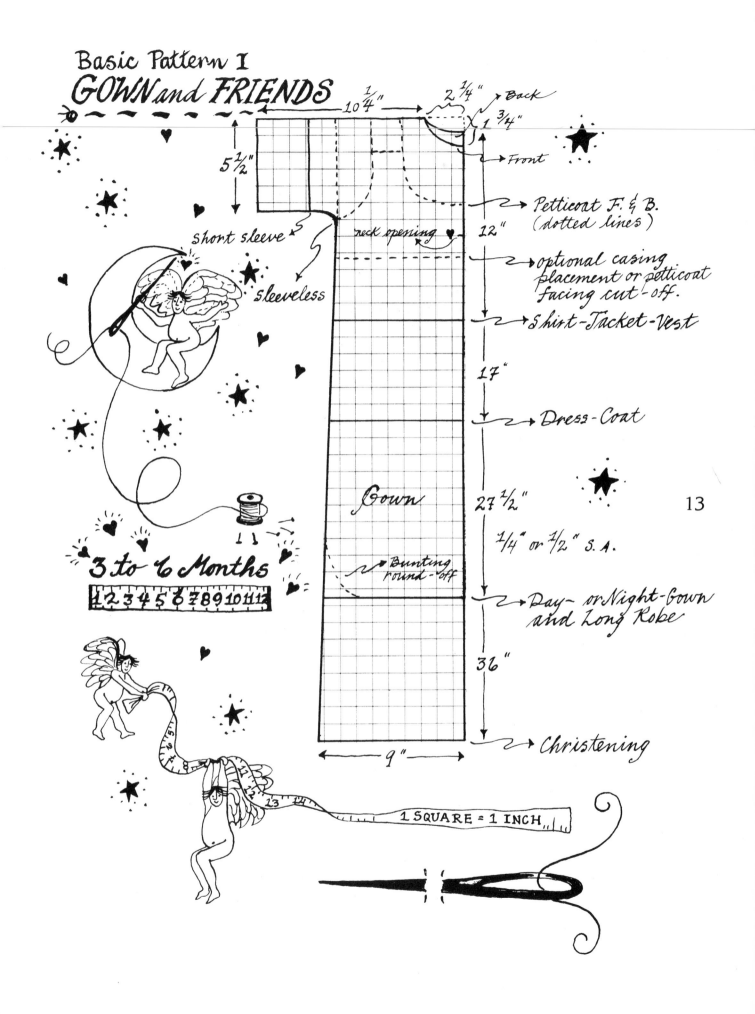

Basic Pattern I
GOWN and FRIENDS

10 1/4"

2 1/4" → Back

1 3/4"

5 1/2"

→ Front

short sleeve

sleeveless

neck opening

Petticoat F. & B.
(dotted lines)

12"

optional casing
placement or petticoat
facing cut-off.

Shirt-Jacket-Vest

17"

Dress-Coat

3 to 6 Months

1 2 3 4 5 6 7 8 9 10 11

Gown

27 1/2"

13

1/4" or 1/2" S.A.

Bunting
round-off

Day- or Night-Gown
and Long Robe

36"

9"

Christening

1 SQUARE = 1 INCH

Basic Pattern I
GOWN and FRIENDS

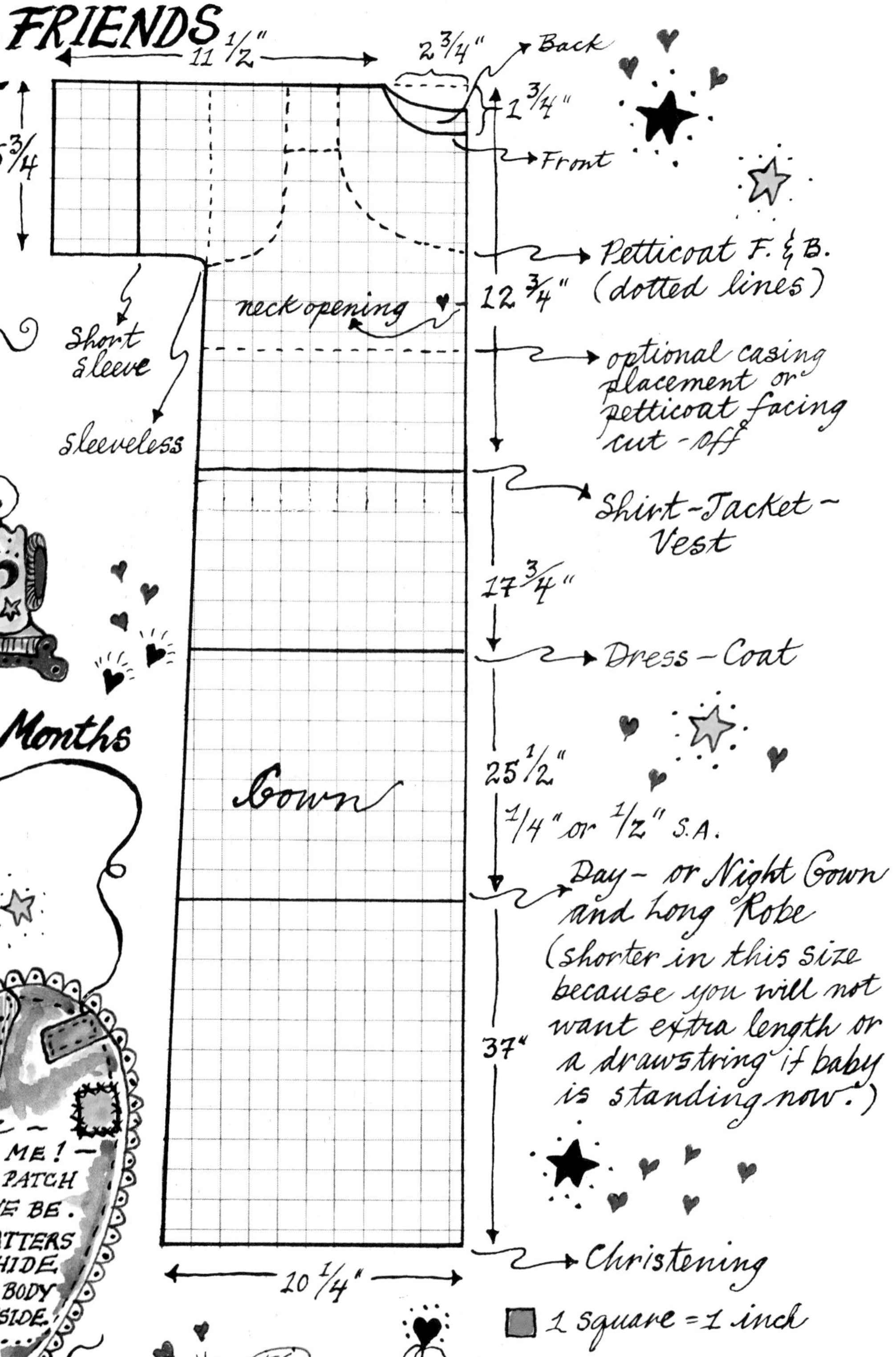

11 1/2"

2 3/4" → Back

5 3/4"

1 3/4"

→ Front

Short sleeve

Sleeveless

neck opening ♥

→ Petticoat F. & B.
(dotted lines)

12 3/4"

→ optional casing placement or petticoat facing cut-off

→ Shirt-Jacket-Vest

17 3/4"

→ Dress-Coat

25 1/2"

Gown

1/4" or 1/2" S.A.

→ Day- or Night Gown and Long Robe
(shorter in this size because you will not want extra length or a drawstring if baby is standing now.)

37"

6 to 12 Months

14

BUT WHAT WE WEAR —
O DEARIE ME! —
IS NAUGHT BUT A PATCH
UPON WHAT WE BE.
AND RAGS AND TATTERS
OFTEN HIDE
A BRAVE LITTLE BODY
BUNCHED UP INSIDE.

WALTER de la MARE

10 1/4"

→ Christening

■ 1 square = 1 inch

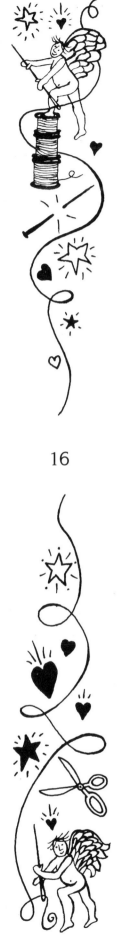

Basic Pattern I:

Home-from-the-Hospital Gown and Hooded Folk Scarf Jacket

This version of the basic gown pattern makes use of a beautiful old cotton eyelet curtain. You could also use other fancy curtains with lace or embroidery, or in any appealing print or weave. You might use an old tablecloth of lightweight linen or cotton, with lace or embroidery, or an old petticoat with all-by-hand whitework embroidery. Or try antimacassars, and doilies, dresser scarves, fancy hand towels and napkins or placemats, handkerchieves, out-of-style party dresses and dressy blouses.

There was enough eyelet edging on this curtain to trim the sleeves and neckline as well as the front and back center hemlines of the illustrated project. A colorful accent is achieved by the insertion of calico side gussets and by pairing the gown with a snuggly hooded jacket made from a tattered worsted folk scarf. Still made in the middle European Slavic countries or the Ukraine, these bright cotton or woolen scarves are often sold in the five-and-dime (in case you are unable to locate one in the thrift store or if there isn't one in the family). Any cotton print scarf—don't overlook bandanas—will work just as well. The worn areas of the scarf were covered very successfully with heart appliques in the calico gusset and jacket lining. The hood is attached to the neckline of the jacket with a series of loops through which a twisted yarn tie (fabric cord or ribbon) can be drawn. This decorative technique allows for removal of the hood if desired. With a layer of polyester quilt batting sandwiched between the scarf fabric and the lining, the jacket is not only soft and snuggly, but very warm.

For this design it is recommended that you do not use French seams on the gown as gussets are easier to insert and the seam binding less bulky with regular right-sides-together seams. The half-inch seam allowances can then be trimmed to one-fourth inch and overcast zigzagged together to finish.

On the jacket, a truly handcrafted look can be achieved by binding the main pieces individually with bright bias tape and then assembling with a contrasting embroidery of herringbone stitch. Any fancy embroidery stitch, such as blanket, feather, or cross, will work just as well. To simplify the design, the jacket and lining can be assembled separately and, with the wrong sides together, treated as one piece, bound around the sleeves, hem, and neckline with tape. You may come up with your own ingenious technique for decorative assembly. As with all the projects in this book, use your own very special imagination!

You will need:

- 1 yard fabric for gown
- 1 yard fabric for lining, gussets, and appliques
- 1 folk scarf, approximately 30" square
- ½ yard polyester quilt batting
- Scraps for appliques
- 3 packages bias single-fold tape (10-12 yards)
- Yarns for twisted ties—or ribbon, bias, or fabric
- 4 to 6 cotton or acrylic mini pom-poms or tassels

Before you begin:

Check the Special Techniques section for: neck and sleeve finishes, herringbone embroidery stitch instructions.

16

Instructions for gown:

1. Cut gussets and heart appliques from jacket lining fabric. Bind the bottom edges of the gussets with bias tape.

2. Place gown pattern on the curtain so eyelet is used to best advantage. Cut out gown, using the short sleeve cut-off. From curtain edging, cut a piece for each sleeve end to use for its edging, adding an extra ¼" at the short sleeve line. With WST, stitch sleeves and edgings with ¼" SA. Trim ⅛" and press open. (The raw SA will be on the right side of the gown.)

3. Applique hearts to front of gown (and anywhere else you wish) as illustrated, or design your own arrangement.

4. Pin in gussets and sew all seams together with ½" SA. Trim to ¼" and finish with a very close machine zigzag.

5. Slash CB 6 to 8" (or CF if you want a front opening). Bind opening with bias tape. Trim neckline ¼" and bind with bias, leaving 6-8" extra tape at each end for ties. Sew ties in on one another as you sew the tape down to the neckline. Cut and sew two more 6-8" ties for the middle of the CB opening. Attach firmly.

6. Cut two pieces of bias tape 9½" long. Press the four end raw edges in to the wrong side (see end of step 2). Pin, then top-stitch, bias tape over exposed seam allowance on each arm. The folded ends should meet at the shoulder-to-wrist seam, making a hole in the casing through which to run a drawstring. (See illustration on page 18.) This technique of seam finish and gown embellishment is used on the gown illustrated with the angel piggy vest in the section on jackets and vests.

7. Make Scandinavian twisted ties to thread through the casings. Instructions for the twisted ties are in the Special Techniques chapter, which begins on page 101.

Instructions for folk scarf jacket:

1. Seam allowances are ¼" for this design. Do not cut the pattern any smaller, though. The extra ¼" is good to have if the jacket will be worn over anything bulkier than the gown.

2. Cut the scarf in half. The corner design of this type of fabric is usually its most attractive feature, so consider using that part of it for the bottom corner edges of the jacket. The corners of the illustrated jacket are rounded off. Place jacket pattern onto scarf as you wish, or use layout shown on page 18. The sleeves may be separated from the body for extra interest in the bias finishing detail. Follow the dotted lines from underarm to shoulder (vest cut-off lines) and move the sleeves over, adding ½" when cutting out.

3. Cut out lining and quilt batting in the same manner.

4. Pin, then machine- or hand-applique hearts over the worn places in your scarf or arrange them according to your own design on the scarf pieces. Press.

5. Sandwich polyester batting between wrong sides of scarf and lining, pin, then zigzag baste together on the edges. If you are going to do hand or machine quilting through the three layers, now is the time to do it.

6. Bind all edges with bias tape, being sure to cover the zigzag basting stitches.

7. Assemble jacket by means of fancy embroidery over seam edges; they should just touch (see the illustration).

8. Cut 17 pieces of bias tape, each 2" long (9 for the jacket neck, 7 for the hood neckline, and 1 for the hood point). Fold them in half lengthwise and stitch closed. Fold them in half to form loops and pin 9 of them evenly spaced along the jacket neckline, and 7 along the hood neckline (see illustration). Do a fine zigzag applique stitch with the machine over the raw edges to secure loops. There are two loops fewer on the hood to allow for a fold-over to show the lining.

9. Make Scandinavian twisted ties or ties of your choice for the neckline and the hood point loop. (See Special Techniques, beginning on page 101.) Secure contrasting or coordinating pom-poms to the ends if desired.

Home-from-the-Hospital Gown:

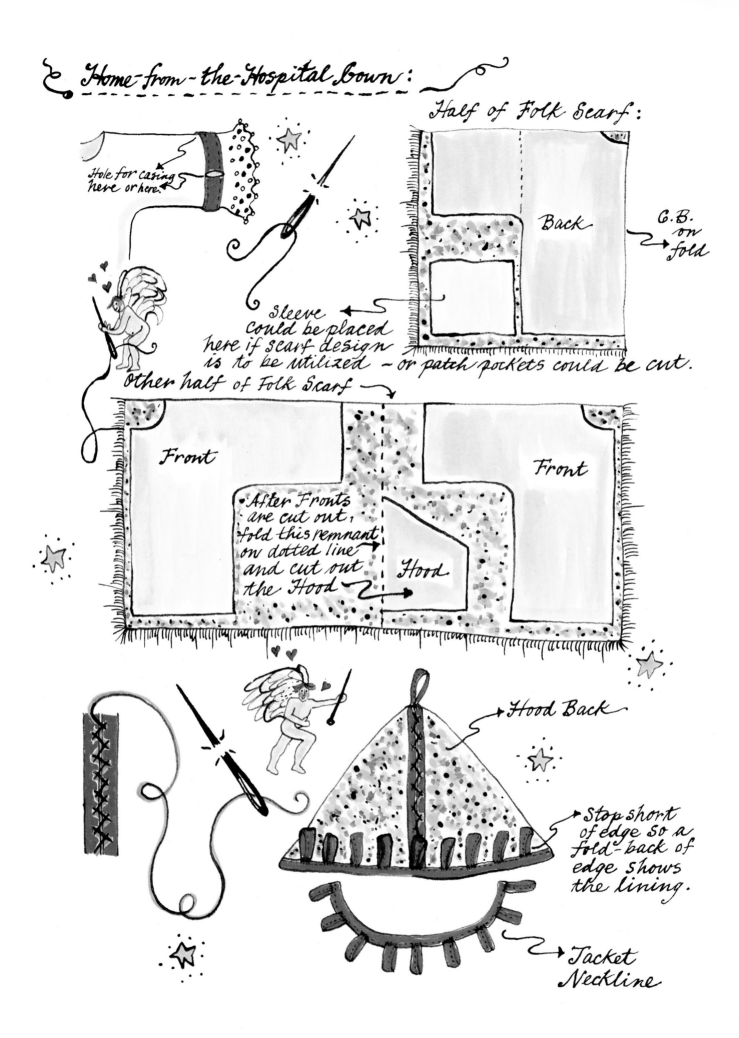

Hole for casing here or here.

Half of Folk Scarf:

Back

C.B. on fold

sleeve could be placed here if scarf design is to be utilized — or patch pockets could be cut.

Other half of Folk Scarf →

Front

Front

After Fronts are cut out, fold this remnant on dotted line and cut out the Hood

Hood

Hood Back

Stop short of edge so a fold-back of edge shows the lining.

Jacket Neckline

Day or Night Gowns:

Be brave: try a black background print:

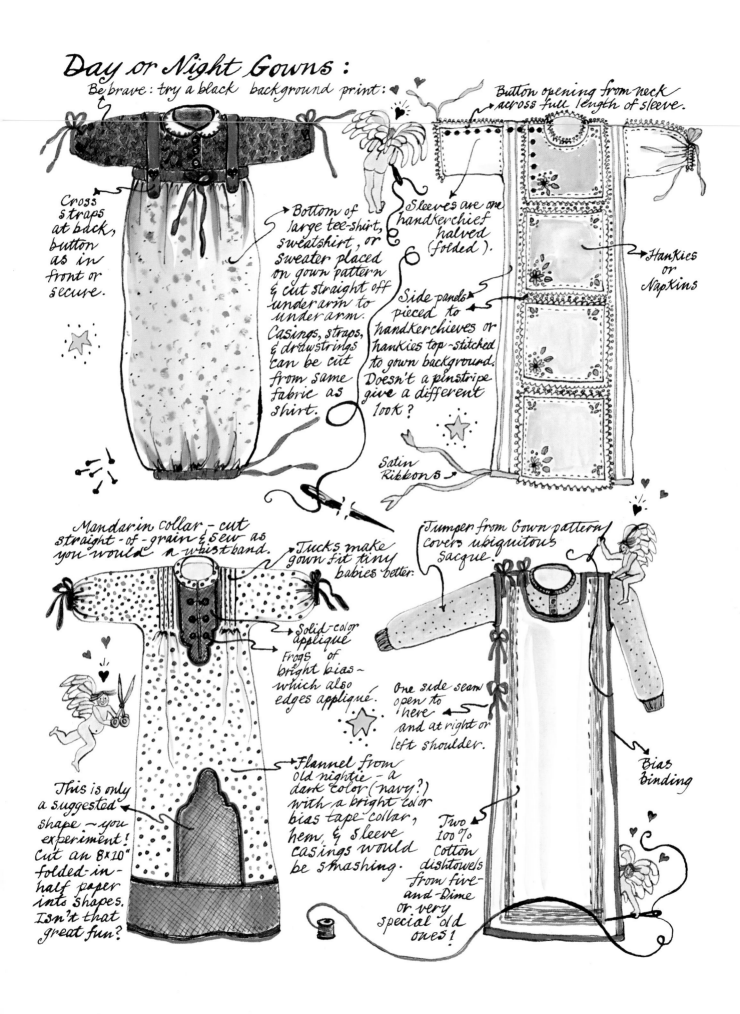

Cross straps at back, button as in front or secure.

Bottom of large tee-shirt, sweatshirt, or sweater placed on gown pattern & cut straight off under arm to under arm. Casings, straps, & drawstrings can be cut from same fabric as shirt.

Button opening from neck across full length of sleeve.

Sleeves are one handkerchief halved (folded).

Side panels pieced to handkerchieves or hankies top-stitched to gown background. Doesn't a pinstripe give a different look?

Hankies or Napkins

Satin Ribbons

Mandarin collar – cut straight-of-grain & sew as you would a waistband.

Tucks make gown fit tiny babies better.

Solid-color appliqué

Frogs of bright bias – which also edges appliqué.

This is only a suggested shape – you experiment! Cut an 8x10" folded-in-half paper into shapes. Isn't that great fun?

Flannel from old nightie – a dark color (navy?) with a bright color bias tape collar, hem, & sleeve casings would be smashing.

Jumper from Gown pattern covers ubiquitous sacque.

One side seam open to here and at right or left shoulder.

Two 100% cotton dishtowels from five-and-dime or very special old ones!

Bias binding

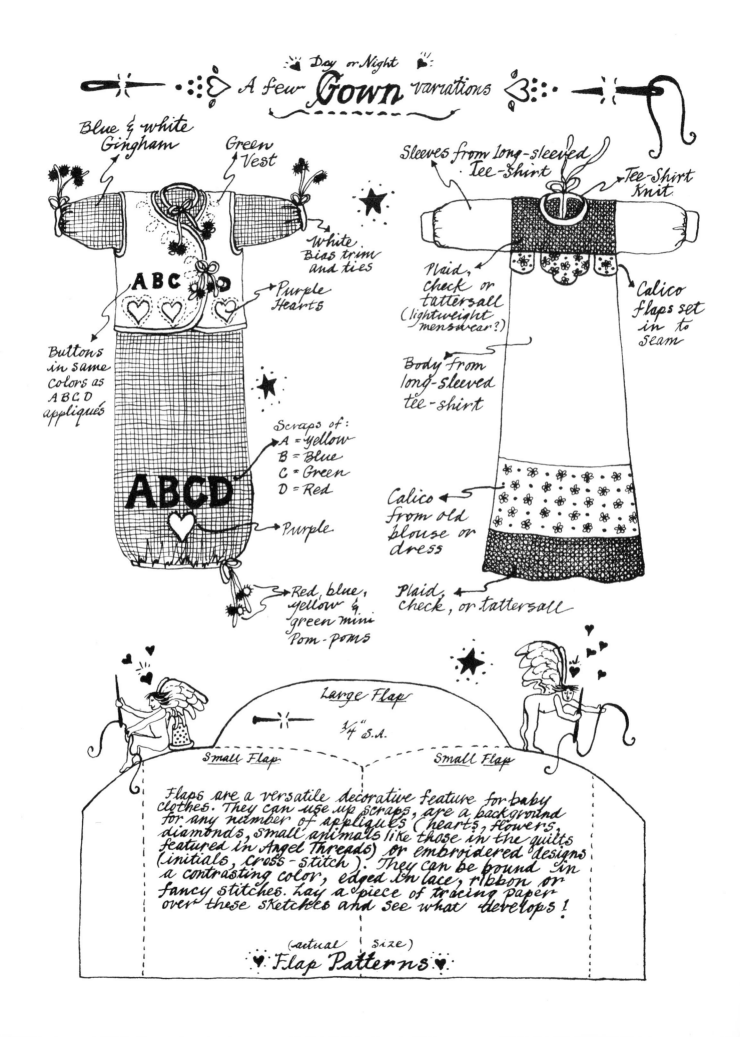

Blue & white Gingham

Green Vest

ABC

White Bias trim and ties

Purple Hearts

Buttons in same colors as A B C D appliqués

ABCD

Scraps of:
A = yellow
B = Blue
C = Green
D = Red

→ Purple.

→ Red, blue, yellow & green mini Pom-poms

Sleeves from long-sleeved Tee-Shirt

Tee-Shirt Knit

Plaid, check or tattersall (lightweight menswear?)

Calico flaps set in to seam

Body from long-sleeved tee-shirt

Calico from old blouse or dress

Plaid, check, or tattersall

Large Flap
¼" S.A.

Small Flap   Small Flap

Flaps are a versatile decorative feature for baby clothes. They can use up scraps, are a background for any number of appliqués (hearts, flowers, diamonds, small animals like those in the quilts featured in Angel Threads) or embroidered designs (initials, cross-stitch). They can be bound in a contrasting color, edged in lace, ribbon or fancy stitches. Lay a piece of tracing paper over these sketches and see what develops!

(actual size)
♥ **Flap Patterns** ♥

Basic Pattern I:
Day or Night Gown

Standard recycling may be the best approach for designing these simple gowns. You could search through your closets for an old favorite but damaged or out-of-style dress, shirt, blouse, skirt, or nightgown. You could use a large apron, a large tee shirt, lightweight sweater or sweatshirt, sheets or pillowcases—anything too nice to give away but no longer wearable. Try combining cotton knits with tiny printed or checked woven fabrics for eye-catching results. Mixed textures and fibers work very nicely for this project as long as they conform to your washing plans. These gowns will be worn often, so you will probably want the care of them to be simple.

The day gown is an easy way to add extra warmth in the winter, because when it's worn over the ubiquitous knit sacque, of which most babies have so many, it adds an extra layer of insulation. In summer it can be cool as a cucumber with the right fabric choices. Even more fun, though, is seeing how exciting your baby can look as you continue to experiment with unusual color and pattern combinations. Open, flapped, or drawstring bottoms give easy access for diaper changing, and the day look is texturally interesting when you add a vest or a tabard to the gown. See that section for design inspiration.

For nightwear the most important considerations are softness, comfort, and, depending on the season, warmth or coolness. Commercially made nightwear and new fabrics are usually tested to meet flammability standards. You will have to decide upon your approach to this issue if the garment you make is to be worn all night.

You will need:

- 1 yard 45" width fabric or the equivalent in smaller pieces to be sewn together
- 3 to 4 packages ½" single-fold bias tape (optional)
- buttons and snaps . . .

   or

   tape, ribbon, bias fabric strips to make ties and drawstrings (your own design will determine what you need)

21

Before you begin:

Refer to the Special Techniques section on page 101 for detailed instructions for: embroidery stitches, sleeve and hem finishes, French seams, collars.

Instructions:

1. Use Basic Pattern I, pages 12-14.

2. Cut out pattern. Experiment with piecing fabrics together in different ways for different looks.

3. If you are going to applique, embroider, or otherwise embellish the gown, you should do so now, before the pattern pieces are assembled. Press.

4. Determine where the gown will open (CF, CB, or a side/shoulder opening) and sew together with French seams. If you want to sew brightly colored bias tape over the seams as in the illustrated gown with angel piggy vest on page 50, the seams should be sewn WST so raw edges are on right side. Trim to ¼", press, and top-stitch bias tape over the seams, turning raw edge ends under as you do so.

5. Finish ends of sleeves. Finish bottom of gown in same manner (if drawstring), or as you wish—deep hem? scalloped edge? trimmed? banded?

6. Apply collar or neckline finish of your choice.

7. Finish neck opening in manner desired (ties, buttons, snaps, frogs).

HOLIDAY DRESS

~ Front ~

fold

white crochet cotton twisted ties

Bunny buttons

tucks to line of sleeve/underarm

C.F. & C.B. seamed – add 1/4" beyond F&B pattern line marked "fold"

white

black embroidery floss knotted & ends left long for whiskers

white collar fabric

Tail could be a pom pom or a circle of fake fleece appliquéd or french knots

~ Back ~

white collar, green blanket stitch & mock tatting

green bias casing

white stars embroidered

red long john knit

green

black trunks embroidered

green bias binding

Moon

Pine Tree

Bunny

Tail

Actual size appliqués

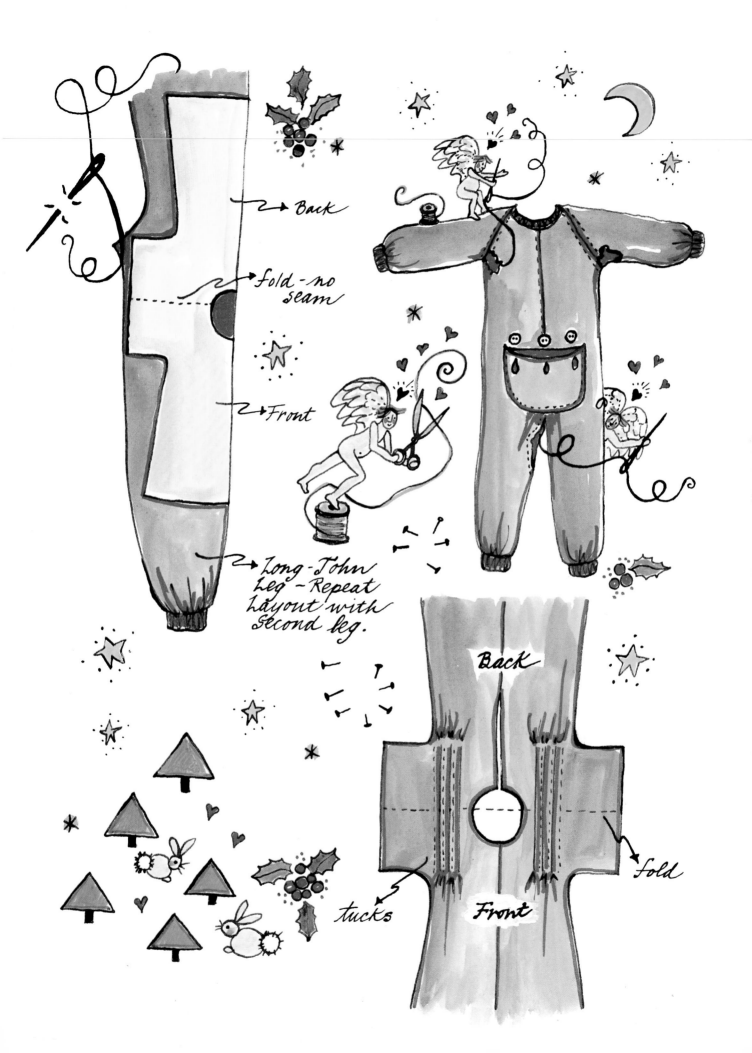

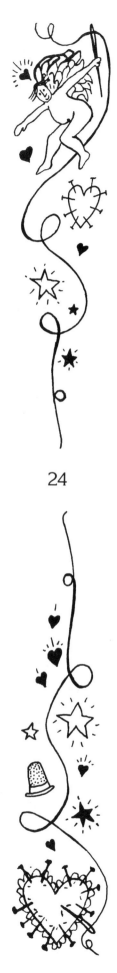

DRESSES

Just imagine how many ways there are to design a dress! The very word "dress" is derived from illustrative words such as "decorate," "trim," "adorn," "display," and "ornament."

A dress from the basic gown pattern can have so many different looks that the list almost defies a limit. Many of the illustrated suggestions are executed by applying textiles on top of a background fabric in a decorative manner. Because the basic pattern has no waistline, you may decide where you wish one to appear.

Picture an applied casing for a drawstring, either narrow or wide, in three different places: above the waist for an Empire look, at the waist for a skirt look, or at the hips for a drop-waisted, 1920's look. Don't be deterred because these terms are used to describe adult styles. Baby clothing throughout history has reflected women's fashion in particular and adult clothing in general. In past centuries, infants and children were dressed as little adults and with no thought of their comfort. You can benefit from the designs of these historical clothes while using the knowledge we've gained in child development studies correlating a baby's happiness with his comfort.

A wonderful source of design inspiration is the costume history section of your local library. Art history books offer a wealth of beautiful paintings which show in lovely detail the exquisite clothing of yesterday's children. Many historical designs lend themselves to adaptation to the simple pattern given here. Explore this avenue and expand your knowledge at the same time!

Holiday Dress

Sometimes the best design ideas take form from something you've been wearing for years. If you enjoy the outdoors even in the coldest of weather, you probably have a pair of those softest-of-soft, warmest-of-warm, Dr. Denton-style red long johns. And if you are like many people who love them, even when the underarm and crotch seams won't take any more mending, you hate to tear them up for dust rags—the fabric is just too smooth from all that wearing.

The red long johns that were used for the holiday dress had enough fabric left in the legs to allow them quite a metamorphosis. They were saved beyond their usefulness because of senti-mentality: the owner was a runner in all sorts of weather and those drawers had kept her warm many a snowy winter morning. Even such a common item as long underwear can have memories attached to it which make it worth re-using!

One of the nicest aspects of this design is its versatility. In red, green and white it certainly plays the Christmas role, but by changing the background to a pastel, it becomes a springtime dress.

Long johns are manufactured in many useful shades and fabric combinations, so whatever you have or find will probably work beautifully. But look, too, for special winter fabrics to recycle, such as velvet or velveteen, flannel, or corduroy (from pants or old skirts?). For summer, try linens, percales, cottons and cotton blends, dimity, chambray (now, don't laugh, but some of the finest chambray to be found today is in men's high-quality boxer shorts!).

You will need:

- 3/4 yard fabric of your choice
- 1/3 yard white fabric for collar and for bunny and moon appliques
- Embroidery floss—green, black and white
- 2 packages green bias tape
- 6 tiny white bunny buttons for front embellishment and back neck opening
- Crochet cotton for twisted ties
- Scrap of fake fleece for tail (optional)

Before you begin:

Note that the line for the dress/coat length on Basic Pattern I is the finished length. If you desire a hem, add two to three inches. Check the Special Techniques section (it begins on page 101) for instructions on the following: sleeve casings, back neck opening, collar application, chain or stem stitch, Scandinavian twisted ties, blanket stitch, mock tatting.

Instructions:

1. Use Basic Pattern I, pages 12-14.

2. Cut out pattern according to layout for working with old long johns (page 23), or however your pattern works best with your chosen fabric. Use the short sleeve cut-off on the pattern.

3. Use a ¼" SA for this project to allow extra room for the shoulder tucks. With RST, sew CF and CB up to neck opening point with a zigzag overcast stitch. Press.

4. Cut out collar and appliques. Sew appliques to the front and back with fine applique zigzag stitch using corresponding colors of thread, following the placement in the illustration.

5. Embroider white stars, black tree trunks, and black whiskers.

6. Pin three ½" tucks across shoulders from armhole to armhole, making them each approximately 9½" long (see illustration). Start 2" in from the neckline for the first one. The second and third are placed ½" from each other. Pin and/or baste, then machine-stitch.

7. Sew arm, underarm, and side seams. Press.

8. Bind bottom of dress with bias tape. Sew sleeve casings.

9. With bias tape, finish back neck opening.

10. With RST, sew the collars together around the outside curve. Then follow collar application directions in Special Techniques section.

11. With green embroidery floss, do a fine blanket stitch around edge of the collar. Then work mock tatting around the edge, using every other blanket stitch as a guide for the tatting loops.

12. Sew on three center front buttons with green embroidery floss, then three center back closure buttons. Make corresponding thread loops along opposite side of CB closure. You may want to place an extra snap or hook and eye fastener at the top of the CB row of buttons.

13. With white crochet cotton, make Scandinavian twisted ties for the sleeve casings.

25

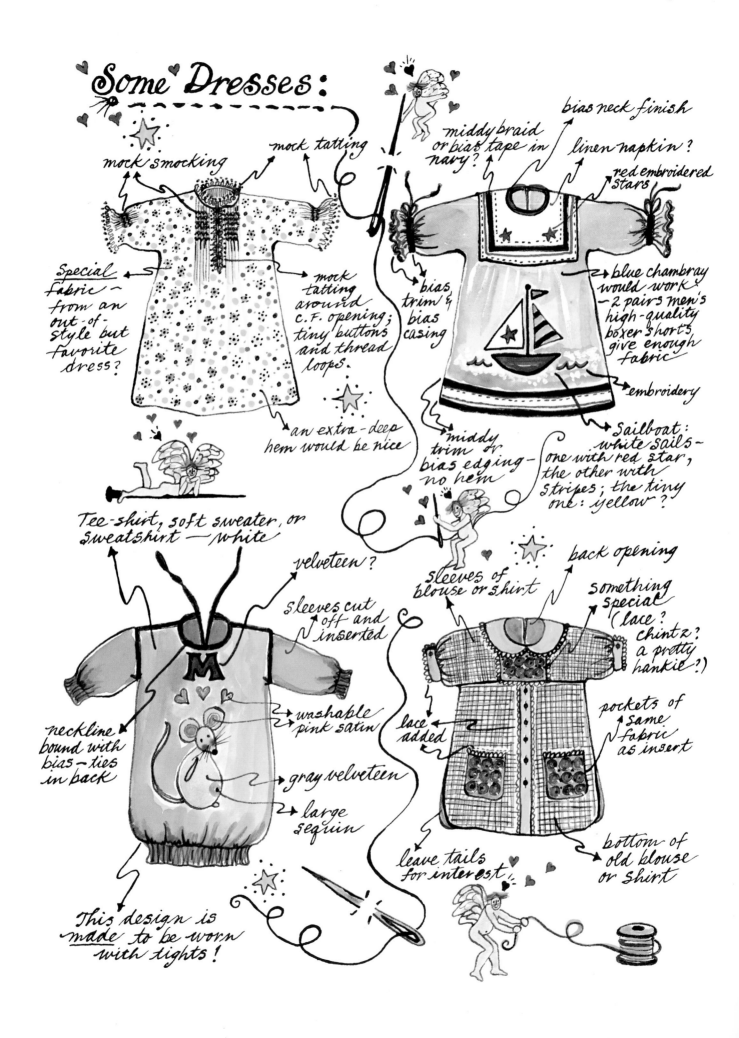

Some Dresses:

mock smocking

mock tatting

Special fabric — from an out-of-style but favorite dress?

mock tatting around c.f. opening; tiny buttons and thread loops

an extra-deep hem would be nice

middy braid or bias tape in navy?

bias neck finish

linen napkin?

red embroidered stars

bias trim & bias casing

blue chambray would work — 2 pairs men's high-quality boxer shorts give enough fabric

embroidery

Sailboat: white sails — one with red star, the other with stripes; the tiny one: yellow?

middy trim or bias edging — no hem

Tee-shirt, soft sweater, or sweatshirt — white

velveteen?

sleeves cut off and inserted

sleeves of blouse or shirt

back opening

something special (lace? chintz? a pretty hankie?)

neckline bound with bias — ties in back

washable pink satin

gray velveteen

large sequin

lace added

pockets of same fabric as insert

bottom of old blouse or shirt

leave tails for interest

This design is made to be worn with tights!

M

Layout for Mock Smocked or Tucked Dress:

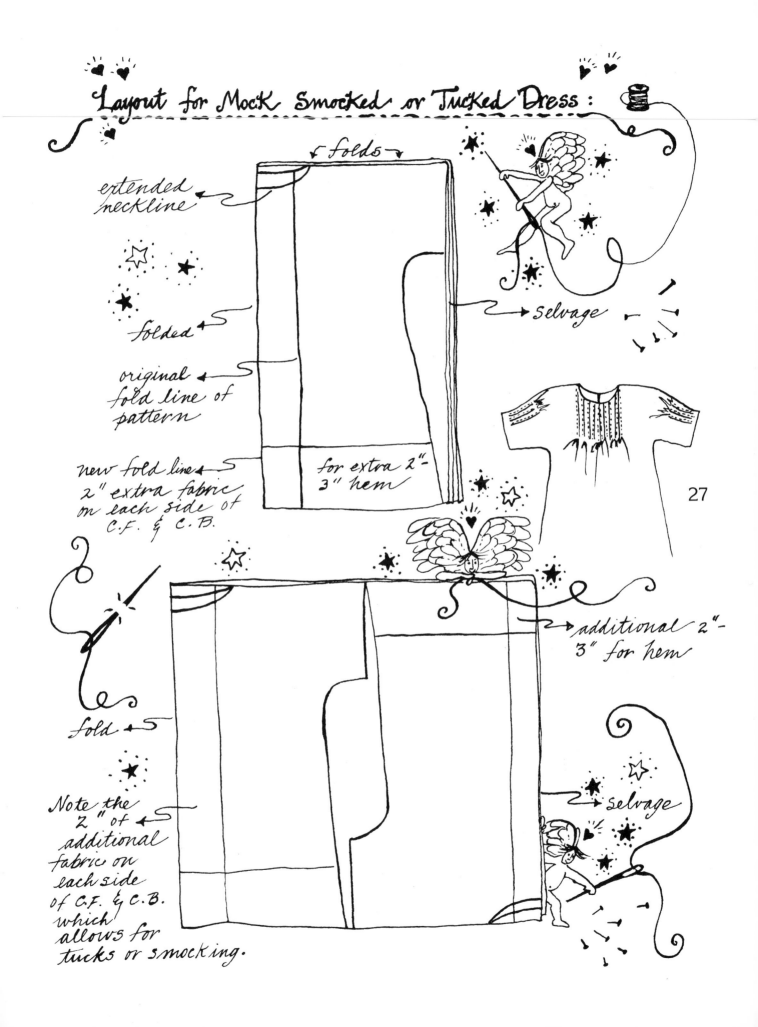

folds

extended neckline

selvage

folded

original fold line of pattern

new fold line 2" extra fabric on each side of C.F. & C.B.

for extra 2"- 3" hem

27

additional 2"- 3" for hem

fold

selvage

Note the 2" of additional fabric on each side of C.F. & C.B. which allows for tucks or smocking.

Basic Pattern I:

Mock Smocked or Tucked Dress

This dress has a timeless appeal—it could have been worn 50 or 60 years ago. In fact, it was designed from a dress that old. The perfect little summer dress, it looks just as charming in warmer fabrics for winter. For a summer weight dress, try satiny-smooth percale, gingham, seersucker, lawn, dimity, batiste, chambray, or pique from all the sources previously discussed. Challis, flannel, and soft pinwale corduroy are a few fabrics that would be good for winter warmth.

Before you begin, check the Special Techniques section for instructions on: mock smocking, mock tatting, bias-faced neckline finish, and center front finish.

You will need:

- ¾ to 1 yard fabric of your choice
- embroidery floss
- 3 to 6 tiny buttons - for front closing

Instructions for mock smocked dress:

1. Use Basic Pattern I, pages 12-14.

2. Pin CF and CB lines of the pattern 2" away from the fold and/or selvage of the fabric (see pattern layout on page 27).

3. If you have chosen the pattern layout which uses a fold at CB, sew the shoulder-to-sleeve seams and the CF up to the neck opening seams with French seams. Press. If you have chosen the pattern layout which uses a fold on the shoulder-to-sleeve "seam" and on the CF and CB, cut the CF neck opening.

4. Starting ½" below the neckline edge on each side of the CF, prepare the 2" extra fabric you have added to the pattern for mock smocking, following instructions in the Special Techniques section. Use a running stitch ¼" long, and do as many rows as you wish, stopping at the line of the underarm.

5. Prepare the additional 4" at the CB in the same manner.

6. Measure 1" up from the center sleeve edge and gather 4" (2" to each side of the center sleeve). Do two rows of mock smocking.

7. Make French seams for the side-to-sleeve seams. Press.

8. Finish the CF opening and neckline with the bias strip technique. Work French knots on the outside bias rolled edge, then do mock tatting around top of neckline rolled edge and around neckline opening.

9. Sew on tiny buttons and make corresponding thread loops.

10. Hand-roll and sew a ¼" hem at sleeve edges. Do mock tatting at the outermost edge.

11. Sew hem.

Instructions for tucked dress:

Follow the instructions for the mock smocked dress, except for steps 3 to 5. Sew the additional 4" of fabric at CF and CB into tiny tucks. Work tucks on the sleeves, too, as shown in the illustration on page 27.

28

Basic Pattern I:

Christening Gown
with bonnet and petticoat

Pull out all your creative stops! This project offers an opportunity to use the very special textile treasures you have inherited or have found over the years and haven't been able to part with. Extravagance and elegance are very easy to achieve using any number of old and new fabrics and trimmings.

Perhaps your family has in its possession an old wedding gown that is too fragile to be used for that purpose again. The most sturdy parts can be gently washed, dried, and applied to the front of a christening gown with stunning results. Or you could try any combinations of the fabrics suggested for the home-from-the-hospital gown. Old and new combine very nicely in the collage concept, so don't be a bit concerned if all of your materials are not of the same vintage, weight, or even hue.

If the gown you envision is going to be all white, or basically white with some soft color accents, every part of the gown needn't match. Different hues of white and off-white add texture and visual interest to the final product. And by all means, don't forget embroidery of your own for this project; the date of the christening and the baby's initials are worth consideration as is the designer's name (yours!). Today's heirlooms which bear the seamstresses' initials and date of completion are far more valuable than are the anonymous ones. Think of future generations wearing the results of your needlework, then make something timeless and exquisite for your angel.

You will need:

- 2½ yards very fine lawn, batiste, cotton percale, dimity, or linen
- 5 to 6 fancy handkerchieves
- 2 large or several small antimacassars or doilies
- approximately 7 yards satin ribbon ⅜ to ⅝" wide
- 1 yard satin ribbon, 2⅜" width, for appliques
- lace scraps
- 5 to 7 yards assorted lace trims
- tiny buttons: 6 to 8 for back opening; 3 or 4 (optional) if you wish to space some down the CF just under the neckline; and 2 to 4 for petticoat shoulders

Before you begin:

Refer to the Special Techniques section, page 101, for instructions for embroidery stitches, mock tatting, French seams, making ribbon casings, and rosettes.

Instructions for christening gown:

1. Use Basic Pattern I, pages 12-14. Cut out gown from background fabric.

2. Sew side seams, using French seams. Press. With the right side of the gown facing you, lay the gown on a table and design your "collage" or follow the design shown on page 31. Pin laces, linens, ribbons, etc., in place, then machine applique, top-stitch, or hand-stitch to the background fabric. Embellish with your own embroidery if you wish. Measure carefully up from the bottom for placement of all pieces.

3. Sew the shoulder-to-sleeve seams, using a French seam. Make a ½" hem, then add a final edging of lace or mock tatting; or do a ribbon casing for a drawstring.

4. With a French seam, sew the CB closed to the point at which you want the opening to end, being careful to match all ribbons, laces, etc., at the seamline. If some discrepancies occur, you might want to consider placing small bows or rosettes on the seams at those spots (these, too, are described in the Special Techniques section).

5. Hem the gown from about 1 to 3" and edge with mock tatting, lace, or ribbon.

6. For the neckline, find the center of a fancy handkerchief and slit open along the dotted line

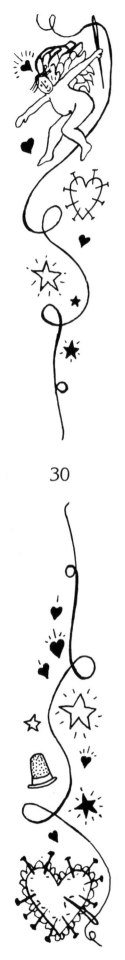

as shown on page 32. Fold the handkerchief over the neckline center. Pin to the front and back of the gown and along the raw edge of the neck opening so that you can cut a neckline in the handkerchief to match that of the gown. If the handkerchief is particularly large, tucks can be sewn by hand or machine to shorten the width across the shoulders, as shown. This extra stitching adds elegance to the yoke which the handkerchief forms, as it is then top-stitched to the gown.

7. Cut from your gown background fabric a bias strip 1¼" wide times the length of the neckline plus 1" (½" turn-under for each end). Bind the neck with this strip, trimming it down if you wish a very tiny rolled edge at the neckline.

8. Finish the CB opening as desired. Refer to the Special Techniques section for some ideas. The illustrated design has tiny buttons and thread loops made in the manner of mock tatting.

9. Sew tiny buttons down CF of yoke.

Instructions for petticoat:

1. Use Basic Pattern I, pages 12-14.

2. The pattern for the petticoat is cut quite long, as extra length under the christening gown is very attractive if special textiles are applied there.

3. Cut out petticoat from same fabric as you have chosen for the gown, or use something which will blend nicely.

4. Sew side seams with French seams after applying any decorations.

5. The necklines and armholes can be finished in different ways. One option is to trim the raw edges ¼" and bind with bias; another is to cut a second front and back, cutting them off at the dotted line marked "casing" on the pattern. Seam the side, then with RST sew around the entire neckline and shoulder straps. Another option is to cut the pattern's seam allowance off and to attach a lace trim with a fine machine zigzag stitch. After one of the first two approaches is executed, a lace trim can be attached by hand or machine as decoration, or embroidery or mock tatting can be used as embellishment.

6. Sew on the tiny buttons at each shoulder and work corresponding buttonholes by hand or machine on the back flap-overs.

7. Hem in any way you wish.

Instructions for bonnet:

1. Use bonnet pattern on page 12.

2. Cut two bonnets, one for the outside and one for the lining. Or, if you are going to incorporate handkerchieves into the bonnet, the lining can be used as a base for placement of the handkerchieves. In this case the lining will have to be turned in to the handkerchief so that no raw edges will show. If you are using the first method, continue:

3. Do a regular ½" seam along the CB of the lining and the outside bonnet fabric. Press open. Run a basting line along each where indicated. With RST, pin and sew around bottom and face the edges, using the same ½" SA. Trim SA to ¼", turn to right side and press.

4. If you have a doily to use for the crown (and it need not be the exact size—extra lace on the edge can add interest if it stands out), gather the machine basting of the bonnet and the crown to 3½" diameter. Turn the edges inside one another and press. Pin together, then blind-stitch closed. Pin doily on as desired and hand sew to outside.

If you do not have a doily to use for the crown, cut out the crown pattern in duplicate. Decorate the outside crown with laces and ribbons, and sew the two pieces together ¼" in from the edge, with WST.

5. Pull the machine basting threads to gather the bonnet back to fit the crown. Turn edges in, and press. Nestle the crown between the bonnet and lining and pin in place. Blind-stitch the bonnet, and then the lining, in place.

6. Cut satin ribbons for ties and hand-sew to the bonnet sides. Cover these points with satin bows or rosettes.

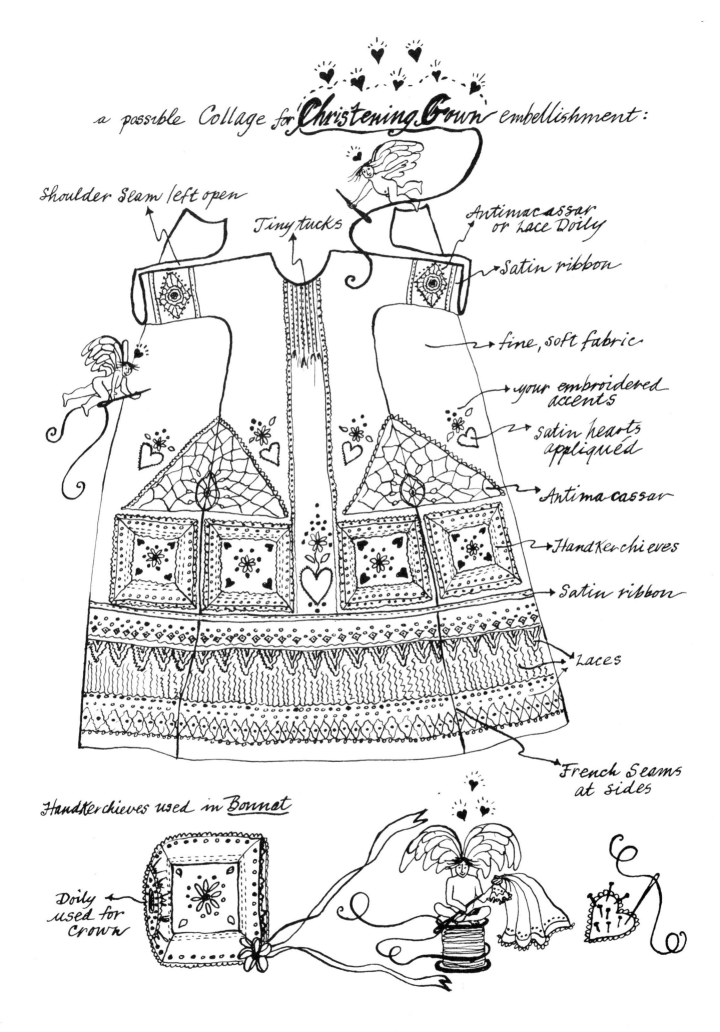

a possible Collage for *Christening Gown* embellishment:

Shoulder Seam left open

Tiny tucks

Antimacassar or Lace Doily

Satin ribbon

fine, soft fabric

your embroidered accents

satin hearts appliquéd

Antimacassar

Handkerchieves

Satin ribbon

Laces

French Seams at sides

Handkerchieves used in Bonnet

Doily used for crown

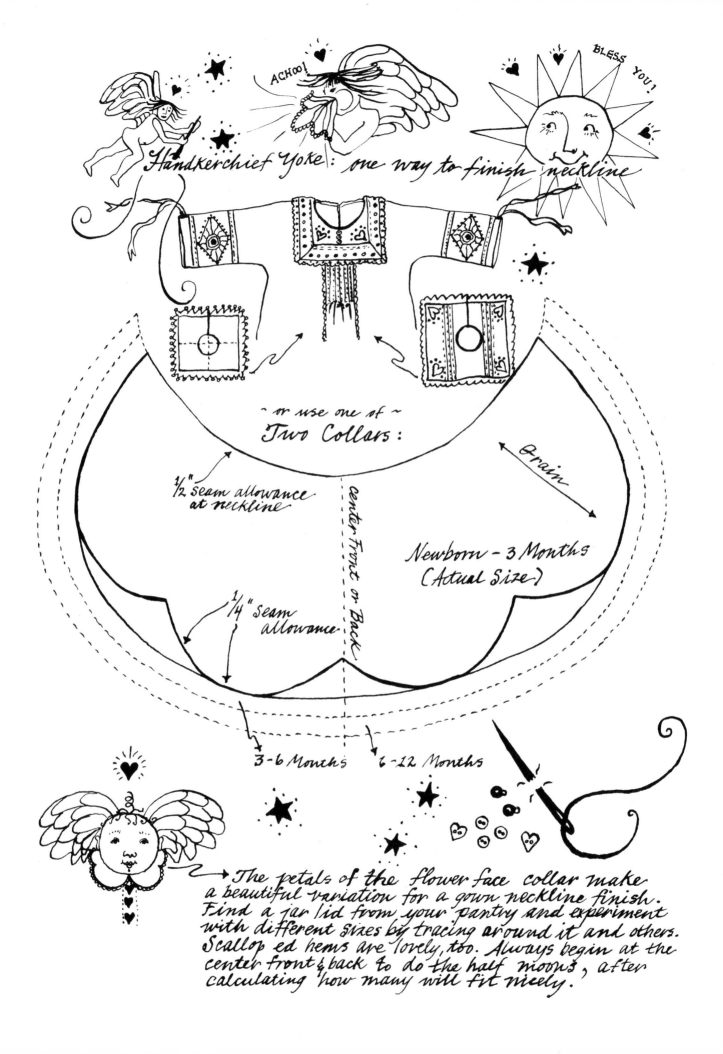

ACHOO!

BLESS YOU!

Handkerchief Yoke: one way to finish neckline

~ or use one of ~
Two Collars:

1/2" seam allowance at neckline

Grain

center front or Back

1/4" seam allowance

Newborn – 3 Months
(Actual Size)

3-6 Months   6-12 Months

→ The petals of the flower face collar make
a beautiful variation for a gown neckline finish.
Find a jar lid from your pantry and experiment
with different sizes by tracing around it and others.
Scalloped hems are lovely, too. Always begin at the
center front & back to do the half moons, after
calculating how many will fit nicely.

Basic Pattern I:
Coats, Robes, and Buntings

The gown pattern becomes a dashing outer garment for special occasions, or a simply splendid bathrobe or fantasy bunting with these variations. The illustrations on the following pages should give you dozens of ideas! Think about the design possibilities of soft corduroy or flannel from old clothing, terry toweling, soft denim from old blue jeans, sweatshirt fabric, or velvet or velveteen from a special dress or jacket. You might consider soft, heavier sweaters, shawls, afghans, or cradle throws, soft blankets or quilted fabrics—perhaps you have one of great-grandmother's quilts which is too tattered in places to use for anything but a very special "little something."

   If you are going to use a heavier fabric, consider using a ¼" seam allowance and finishing with a machine overcast zigzag, or lining the robe instead of using French seams. The result will be a less bulky garment with a roomier fit; this is especially recommended for the buntings. Cut the patterns out as drawn; do not cut down ¼". If you decide to experiment with an old sweater or knit afghan, use the method described in the Special Techniques section (beginning on page 101) for incorporating old knits into your designs.

   To make a robe, follow the directions for the day or night gowns (page 21), unless you are planning to insert linings. In that case, follow the directions for the bunting. The bunting really calls for a lining. If the outer fabric is warm, a soft, lightweight lining fabric will be right; if you choose a lightweight outside fabric, as in the angel-clown illustration, you would want something warm for the lining. A quilted piece—even an old mattress pad would work well—is a good choice for a lightweight outer fabric.

You will need:

- 1 yard outer bunting fabric
- 1 yard lining
- 1 36" separating zipper

   or

   1 36" regular neckline zipper

- pom-poms, buttons, ribbons, or trimmings of your choice

Before you begin:
Refer to the Special Techniques section, page 101, for detailed instructions for seams, hems, and neckline finishes.

Instructions for bunting:

1. Use Basic Pattern I, pages 12-14.

2. Cut out pattern pieces for gown F and B, following dotted lines for sleeveless version. If you do want sleeves, as shown on the moon-and-stars bunting on page 34, cut the back sleeve approximately 2 to 3 inches longer for a flap.

3. Do any applique work before the seams are sewn. Press.

4. Sew with ¼" SA, RST, except for lining CF. Press open on WS.

5. Apply zipper in CF seam of outer bunting. Use a separating zipper if you're making a bunting with a lower back fold-over, otherwise use a neckline zipper.

6. Pin lining and bunting together, WST, and blind-stitch lining to zipper on WS, turning in ¼" SA as you do.

7. Finish the neckline in any way you choose.

8. If you wish to add a matching bonnet or hood, follow instructions on pages 16-17.

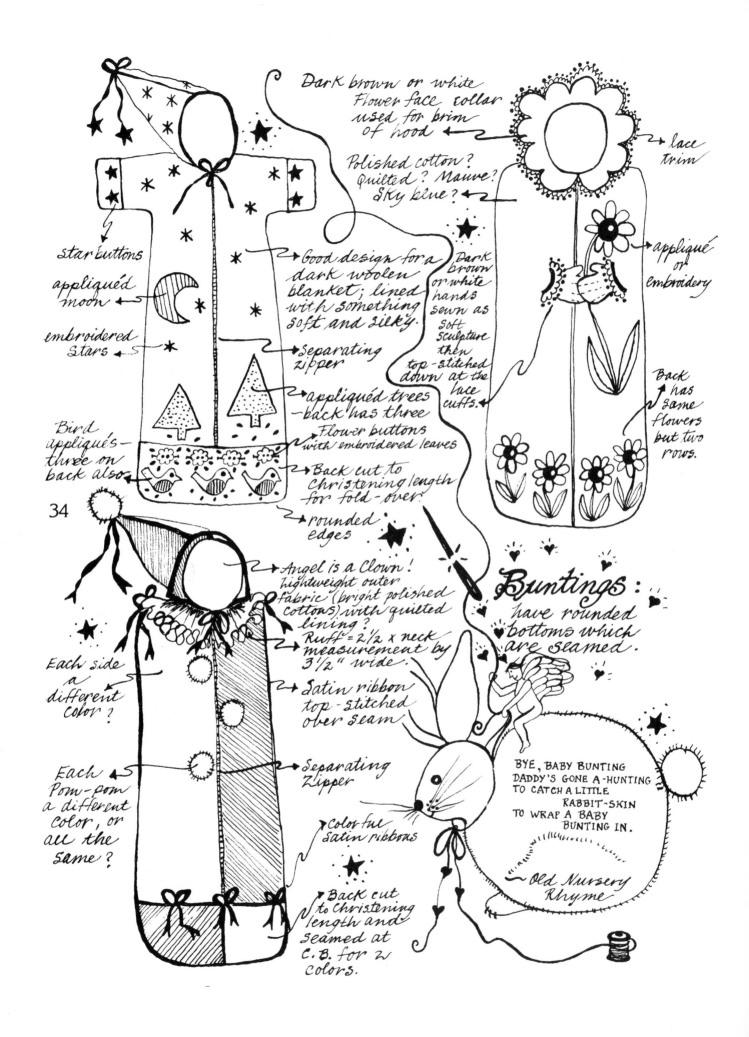

Dark brown or white
Flower face collar
used for brim
of hood →

→ lace
trim

Polished cotton?
Quilted? Mauve?
Sky blue? →

Dark
brown
or white
hands
sewn as
soft
sculpture
then
top-
stitched
down
at the
lace
cuffs. →

star buttons

appliquéd
moon →

embroidered
stars ←

Bird
appliqués—
three on
back also ←

34

→ Good design for a
dark woolen
blanket; lined
with something
soft and silky.

→ Separating
zipper

→ appliquéd trees
—back has three
Flower buttons
with embroidered leaves

→ Back cut to
Christening length
for fold-over.

→ rounded
edges

→ appliqué
or
embroidery

Back
has
same
flowers
but two
rows.

Angel is a Clown!
→ lightweight outer
fabric (bright polished
cottons) with quilted
lining?
→ Ruff = 2½ × neck
measurement by
3½" wide.

→ Satin ribbon
top-stitched
over seam

→ Separating
Zipper

→ Colorful
satin ribbons

→ Back cut
to Christening
length and
seamed at
C.B. for 2
colors.

Each side
a
different
color? ←

Each
Pom-pom
a different
color, or
all the
same?

Buntings :
have rounded
bottoms which
are seamed.

BYE, BABY BUNTING
DADDY'S GONE A-HUNTING
TO CATCH A LITTLE
RABBIT-SKIN
TO WRAP A BABY
BUNTING IN.

~ Old Nursery
Rhyme

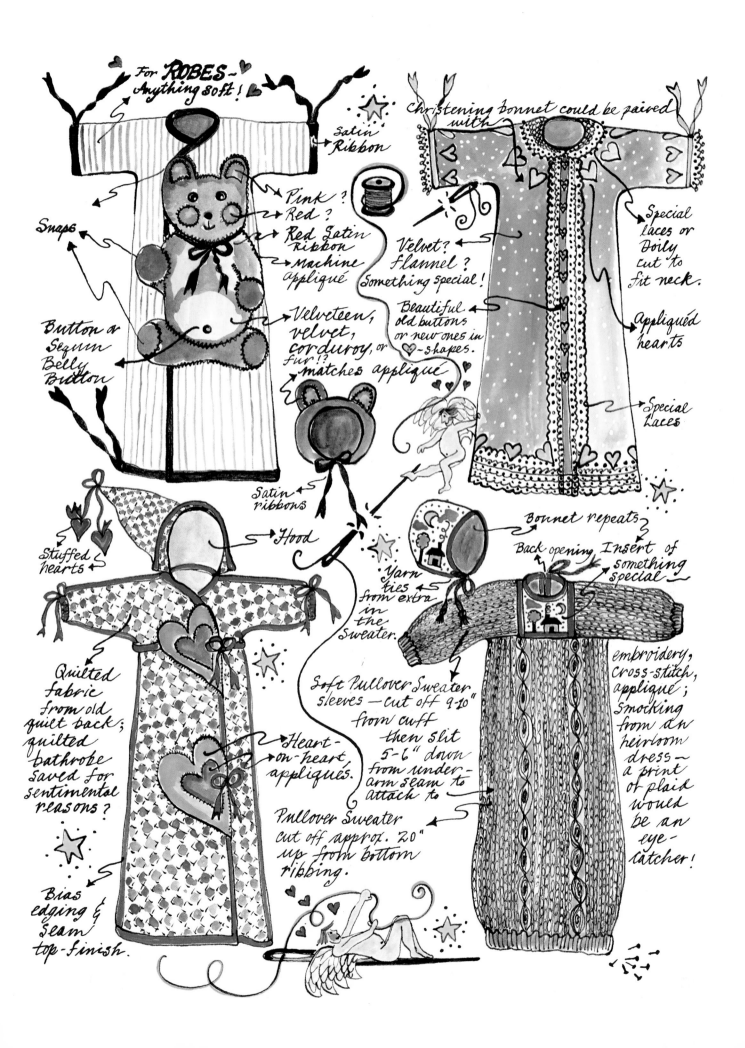

For **ROBES** — Anything soft! ♥

Satin Ribbon

Pink?
Red?
Red Satin Ribbon
machine appliqué

Snaps

Button or Sequin Belly Button

Velveteen, velvet, corduroy, or fur!? matches appliqué

christening bonnet could be paired with

Velvet? flannel? Something special!

Beautiful old buttons or new ones in ♥-shapes.

Special laces or Doily cut to fit neck.

Appliquéd hearts

Special Laces

Satin ribbons

Hood

Stuffed hearts

Quilted fabric from old quilt back; quilted bathrobe saved for sentimental reasons?

Heart-on-heart, appliqués.

Yarn ties from extra in the Sweater.

Soft Pullover Sweater sleeves — cut off 9-10" from cuff then slit 5-6" down from under-arm seam to attach to

Pullover Sweater cut off approx. 20" up from bottom ribbing.

Bias edging & Seam top-finish.

Bonnet repeats

Back opening   Insert of something special

embroidery, cross-stitch, appliqué; smocking from an heirloom dress — a print or plaid would be an eye-catcher!

COATS AND JACKETS

You have already seen one adaptation of this variation of the gown pattern: the folk scarf jacket shown over the home-from-the-hospital gown on pages 15-18. The illustrations on page 43 will provide you with some other design ideas.

For the most part, the coats and jackets illustrated are for cool or cold weather, therefore the fabrics should be chosen accordingly. You can, however, use anything you wish for a look that is unique. Be inspired: any fabric can be insulated for warmth with batting sandwiched behind it. So as long as it fits your cleaning requirements, it will work.

Look for wool or woolen-blend blankets, quilts, mattress pads, tartan, tweed and challis scarves. Consider velvets and velveteens, men's and women's pants and skirts. And how lucky you are, should you be the owner of a less-than-mint-condition ancestral paisley shawl that can be patched together for a beautiful outer garment! Can't you see it trimmed in velvet or velveteen?

If you use heavy or padded fabric, add an extra ¼" all the way around all pattern pieces when you lay out your pattern for cutting. For a coat, you want extra roominess to accommodate the extra bulk on baby (sweater or light jacket underneath) and a lining—which you will in most cases choose to insert.

The illustrated blanket jacket is made of a dusty pink, heavy wool blanket, appliqued with cotton calico hearts and circles from scraps. One of the fabrics used for the hearts was repeated as the lining. Here, the coat pattern was shortened to vest length and narrowed to a width between tabard and vest width for a snug fit.

Blanket Jacket and Crocheted Hat

You will need:

36

- ½ yard blanket wool for jacket or ¾ yard blanket wool for coat
- ½ or ¾ yard calico lining
- calico scraps for appliques
- 1 skein 3-ply (sport weight) yarn for Scandinavian twisted ties, jacket crochet trim, and crocheted hood; or use yarn from your scrap supply
- 10 buttons (Tyrolean pewter hearts were used for the jacket illustrated) - 5 for back closure, 3 to embellish three small appliqued hearts on jacket front, and 2 to embellish hearts on the crocheted hood

  or

  9" separating zipper
- size H crochet hook
- size 0 or 00 crochet hook
- tapestry needle
- approximately 12 mini pom-poms (optional)

Before you begin:

Read the following directions in the Special Techniques section: blanket stitch, single crochet, buttonholes in single crochet, Scandinavian twisted ties.

Instructions for blanket jacket:

1. Use Basic Pattern I pages 12-14.

2. Cut out pattern from the blanket and lining fabric according to the pattern layout on page 39, making sure you cut the F neck lower than the B neck. Decide whether you want to cut the sleeves as separate pieces. If so, the project will be more time-consuming but will be richer in appearance because of the extra crochet work where sleeves are seamed to jacket bodice.

3. Cut appliques from lining fabric and scraps. The illustrated project uses the lining calico for the large CF heart (actual-size pattern on page 39). The oval medallion which appears between the CF large heart and center circle is cut of blanket wool.

4. On the machine, applique the hearts and circles to the blanket following the placement on the illustration or to your choosing.

5. Thread top of machine with thread to match blanket wool, and bobbin with thread to match to lining; baste blanket and lining together with machine zigzag around all edges of all pieces.

6. Yarn edging may be applied in two different ways:
> With a darning needle, do blanket stitch at ⅛" to ¼" spacing all the way around all pattern pieces,
> or
> With steel crochet hook (0 or 00), just above the zigzag basting, punch through blanket and lining and edge all pattern pieces with single crochet. You need strong hands for this, but the result is nice. If you have a wooden crochet hook, you could sharpen the end for easier punching. If the jacket is unlined, the metal one will punch through the blanket without any trouble.

Whichever method you choose, take care to completely cover the machine zigzag basting.

7. With yarn and tapestry needle, join shoulder seams of jacket and sleeves from underarm to underarm. Then the sleeve underarm side seams and jacket side seams in the same manner.

8. At the CB opening, on each edge do two rows of SC with the H hook. On one side work 5 evenly-spaced buttonholes in the second row.

9. Work Scandinavian twisted ties for decorating bottom sleeve edges where cuff turns up (as pictured). Tie on mini pom-poms if desired.

10. Cuffs can be rolled back to show off the lining.

Instructions for crocheted hat:

1. Cut a paper pattern of the hood (pattern on page 12, layout on page 39). Lay it out on a table or in your lap in front of you to enable you to crochet exactly to the pattern size. The instructions given are for size 12 months, so the number of stitches you chain will depend upon the size hood you are making, and on the tension of your work.

2. With size H crochet hook, chain 44. Do 18 rows of SC or work until hood measures 5" from point A to B. Decrease 1 or 2 stitches at each end, following paper pattern for a smooth line from point B to C, until a single stitch remains on hook. Tie off, leaving a strand of yarn long enough to sew back of hood closed.

3. Before sewing hood, pin, baste, then machine-applique calico hearts to "ear" corners of hood, approximately 2" up from each corner. See illustration. Sew a heart-shaped button at the top center of each calico heart.

4. Sew hood back closed from wrong side, using remaining long strand of yarn. Weave yarn end through wrong side of seam and cut off.

5. Make one Scandinavian twisted tie to thread through neck edge, and another small one to use as a tie at the hood point. Sew mini pom-poms to the ends of the neckline tie, at the "ear" corners, and at the hood point, if desired.

~BACK~
~BLANKET JACKET~
WITH HOOD OR CROCHETED HAT

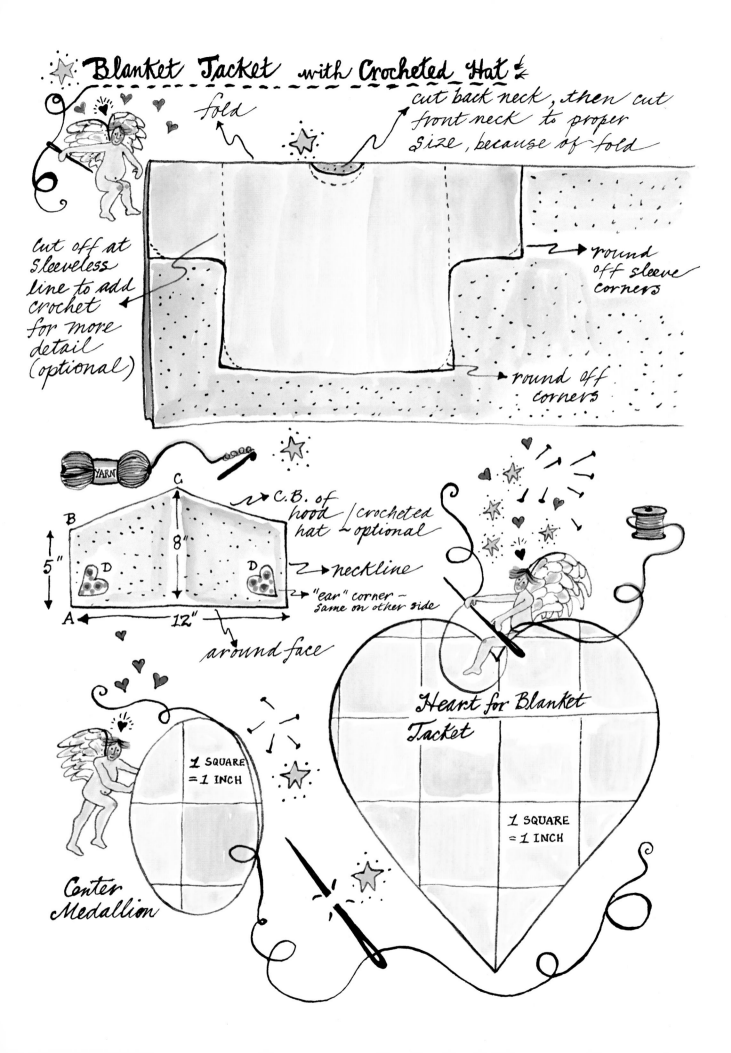

Blanket Jacket with Crocheted Hat

fold

cut back neck, then cut front neck to proper size, because of fold

cut off at sleeveless line to add crochet for more detail (optional)

round off sleeve corners

round off corners

YARN

C
B
D
A
8"
5"
12"

C.B. of hood / crocheted hat ~ optional

neckline

"ear" corner ~ same on other side

around face

Heart for Blanket Jacket

1 SQUARE = 1 INCH

Center Medallion

1 SQUARE = 1 INCH

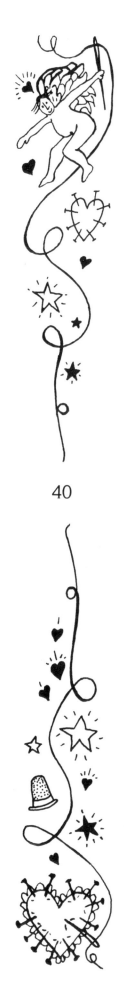

Basic Pattern I:

Caped Coat and Matching Bonnet

This elegant and very old-fashioned design is probably most effective worked up in the two larger-sized patterns. We used an old pair of pinwale corduroy slacks in a floral print. A lining of a silky or satin fabric can be added, and cording, bias binding, piping or middy braid make wonderful accents.

You will need:

- 1 pair of corduroy pants, or 1 yard of 45" lightweight corduroy or wool
- 1 yard lining fabric
- 3 packages single-fold bias tape
- 3 packages middy braid
- 10 to 12 buttons—8 for coat, 4 for sleeves
- 4 to 6 snaps, for extra grip at CF
- white linen for cape: a napkin at least 8" square or an old tablecloth

Instructions:

1. Use Basic Pattern I, pages 12-14.

2. If you are using an old pair of pants, open all seams and press pieces flat. Lay pant legs on cutting surface with RST. Being careful to watch grainline (the curve of the legs fools the eye) and consistent nap direction on all pieces, place paper pattern pieces onto pant legs as shown in the layout or in a way which works best for your particular fabric.

3. Cut out 2 fronts, 2 backs, 4 sleeves, 4 collars. Use the collar pattern shown for the christening gown (page 32) and cut down to a CB depth of about 2 inches—a narrower collar is more effective with the largeness of the cape. Cut 2 bonnet pieces and 1 bonnet crown.

4. Cut out the same pieces, except collar, from lining fabric of your choice.

5. On each front piece, sew middy braid as illustrated.

6. Cut out the cape as in layout. Cut open the CF. Bind with bias tape, or hem, or embroider, or loop middy braid and top-stitch in place as illustrated. Use any embellishment you wish so the cape will be the focal point of the coat. Press.

7. Seam the sleeves together at the arm tops and press. Embellish cuffs with braid.

8. Treat the coat and the lining as two separate coats. With RST, sew the seams with ¼ to ½" seam allowance (depending on how roomy you want the coat to be) and press open.

9. With WST, put lining into coat and pin together down CF and around sleeves. Bind sleeves, CF, and bottom with bias tape, if that is the finish you have decided to use.

10. With WST, baste collars together as close to the edge as possible. Bind edge with bias tape. Top-stitch middy braid to right side in a design if the collar is wide enough, otherwise leave as the illustration shows. Press.

11. Pin cape to coat and machine-baste ¼" from edge. Pin collar to coat, machine-baste in the same manner. Trim SA to ⅛".

12. Finish raw edge of neck with bias tape as outlined in the Special Techniques section.

13. Sew middy braid to very edge of bias tape binding at CF of cape, making evenly spaced button loops down one side as you sew.

14. Sew buttons on the opposite side of cape, and decorative buttons across from loops on the same side for a double-breasted look.

15. Sew large snaps down the wrong side of coat to secure.

16. Make bonnet according to instructions for christening bonnet, page 30. Embellish with bias tape and/or middy braid as in the illustration, or to suit your fancy.

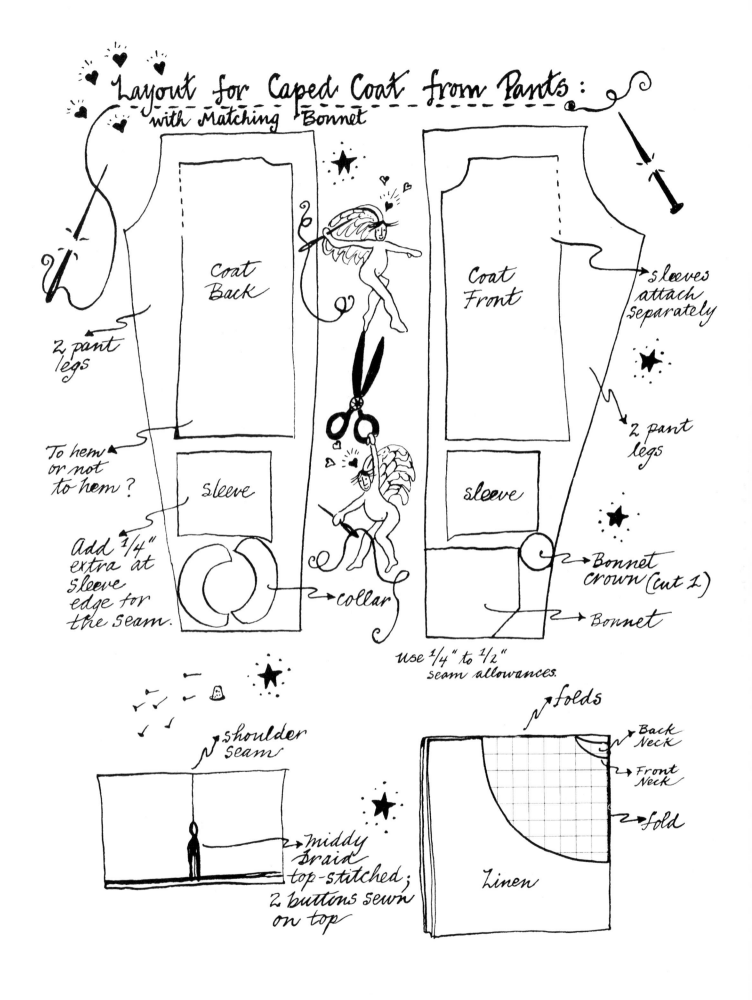

Layout for Caped Coat from Pants:
with Matching Bonnet

Coat Back

2 pant legs

To hem or not to hem?

Add 1/4" extra at sleeve edge for the seam.

sleeve

Coat Front

sleeves attach separately

2 pant legs

sleeve

collar

Bonnet crown (cut 1)

Bonnet

Use 1/4" to 1/2" seam allowances.

shoulder seam

middy braid top-stitched; 2 buttons sewn on top

folds

Back Neck

Front Neck

fold

Linen

MIDDY BRAID CUT! RIP!

CAPED COAT AND MATCHING BONNET

Emily Dickinson:
HOW FITS HIS UMBER COAT COMBINED WITHOUT A
THE TAILOR SEAM, LIKE RAIMENT
OF THE NUT, OF A DREAM.

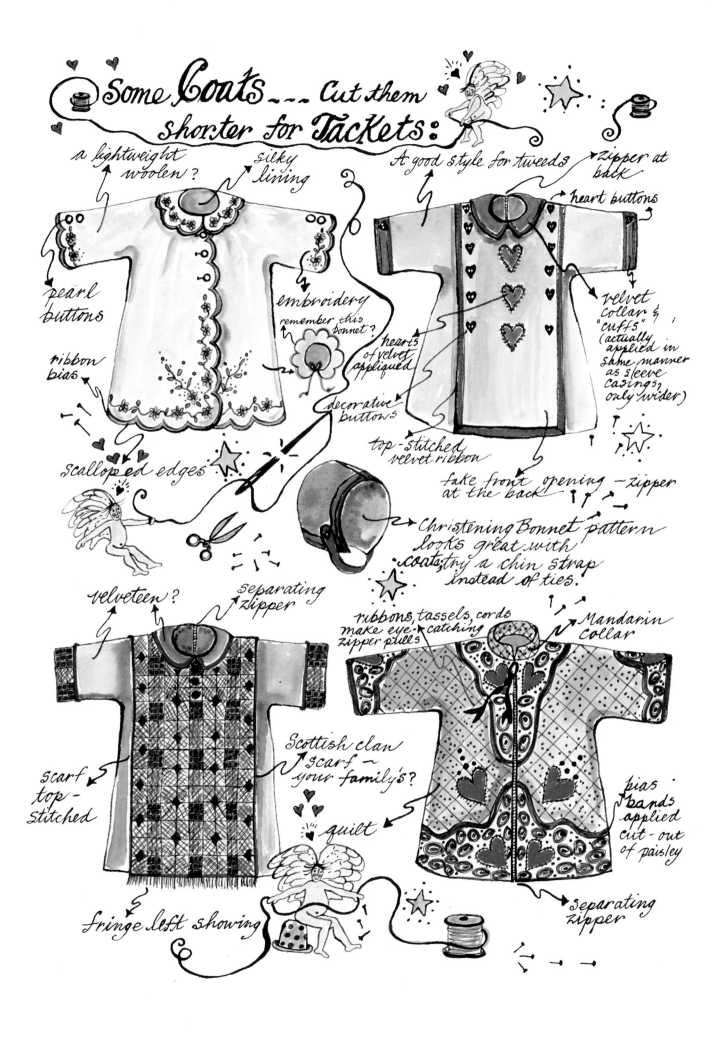

Some Coats... Cut them shorter for Jackets:

a lightweight woolen?

silky lining

A good style for tweeds

zipper at back

heart buttons

pearl buttons

embroidery remember this bonnet?

hearts of velvet appliquéd

velvet collar & "cuffs" (actually applied in same manner as sleeve casings, only wider)

ribbon bias

decorative buttons

top-stitched velvet ribbon

scalloped edges

fake front opening — zipper at the back

Christening Bonnet pattern looks great with coats; try a chin strap instead of ties.

velveteen?

separating zipper

ribbons, tassels, cords make eye-catching zipper pulls

Mandarin collar

Scottish clan scarf — your family's?

scarf top-stitched

quilt

bias bands applied cut-out of paisley

fringe left showing

separating zipper

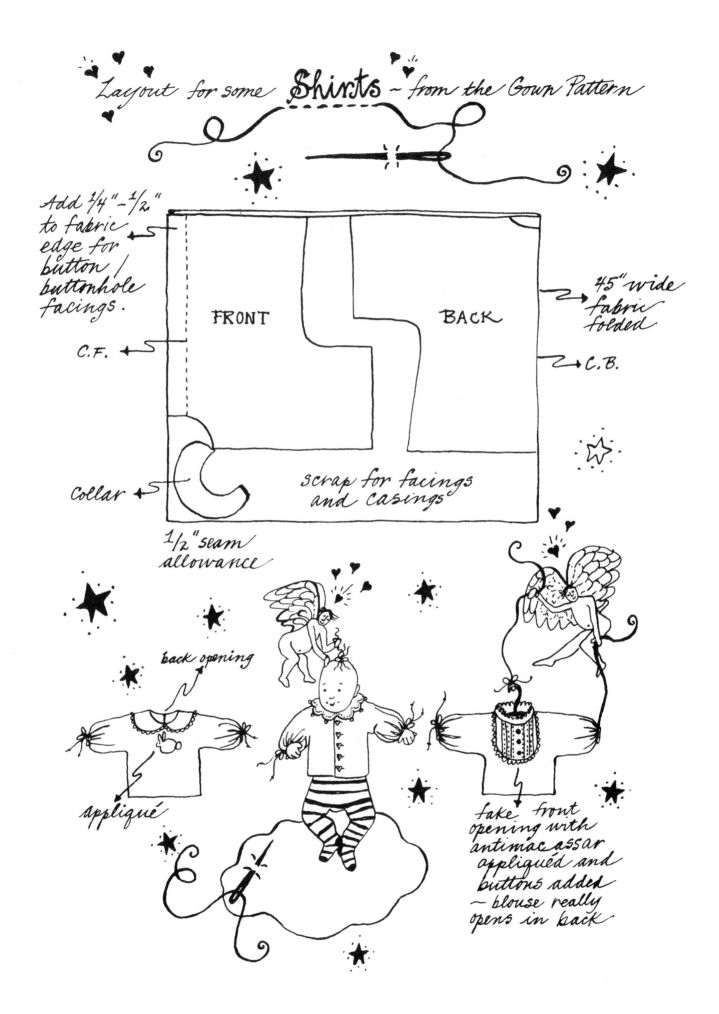

Layout for some **Shirts** ~ from the Gown Pattern

Add ⅟₄" - ½" to fabric edge for button / buttonhole facings.

FRONT

BACK

C.F.

45" wide fabric folded

C.B.

Collar

scrap for facings and casings

½" seam allowance

back opening

appliqué

fake front opening with antimacassar appliquéd and buttons added ~ blouse really opens in back

SHIRTS

A wide range of looks can be achieved with an enchanting shirt. The fabric, trims, and buttons you choose for your shirt will make even a very ordinary pair of, say, tee shirt "sleeve pants" something very special.

The fabric you choose can be anything soft. Small-scale prints, checks, plaids, or stripes are always good choices. Think about collars and casings in contrasting colors for splash if the pants to be worn with the shirt are not the most interesting. Or play down the shirt if the pants are really unique.

If the shirt will open down the front, place the CF pattern edge ¼" to ½" away from the fabric edge to allow extra fabric for the button and buttonhole closing as shown on the layout. If the opening will be in the back you can finish it in the same manner as the front, or just cut the pattern as drawn, without adding fabric for buttons and buttonholes, and bind the edge for snaps or ties. The Special Techniques section, beginning on page 101, explains these techniques fully.

You will need:

- ¾ yards fabric
- 4 to 6 buttons or snaps
- 1 to 2 packages bias tape (optional)

Before you begin:

Study the following in the Special Techniques section: collar applications, neckline finishes, CF and CB finishes, sleeve casings.

Instructions:

1. Use Basic Pattern I, pages 12-14.

2. Pin pattern onto fabric as layout suggests or in the way that best suits your fabric. Be sure to follow the grainline.

3. Cut out. Sew French seams at shoulders and sides.

4. Sew casings onto sleeves.

5. Apply collar or neck finish of your choice.

6. Face the CF or CB, depending on where the shirt opens.

7. Sew evenly spaced buttons on the right front for a boy's shirt, or left front for a girl's. Work corresponding buttonholes.

8. Machine-stitch a very narrow roll-over hem around the bottom of the shirt.

9. Make drawstrings for the sleeve casings from shirt fabric or bias tape, or crochet cotton twisted ties. Thread them through the casings.

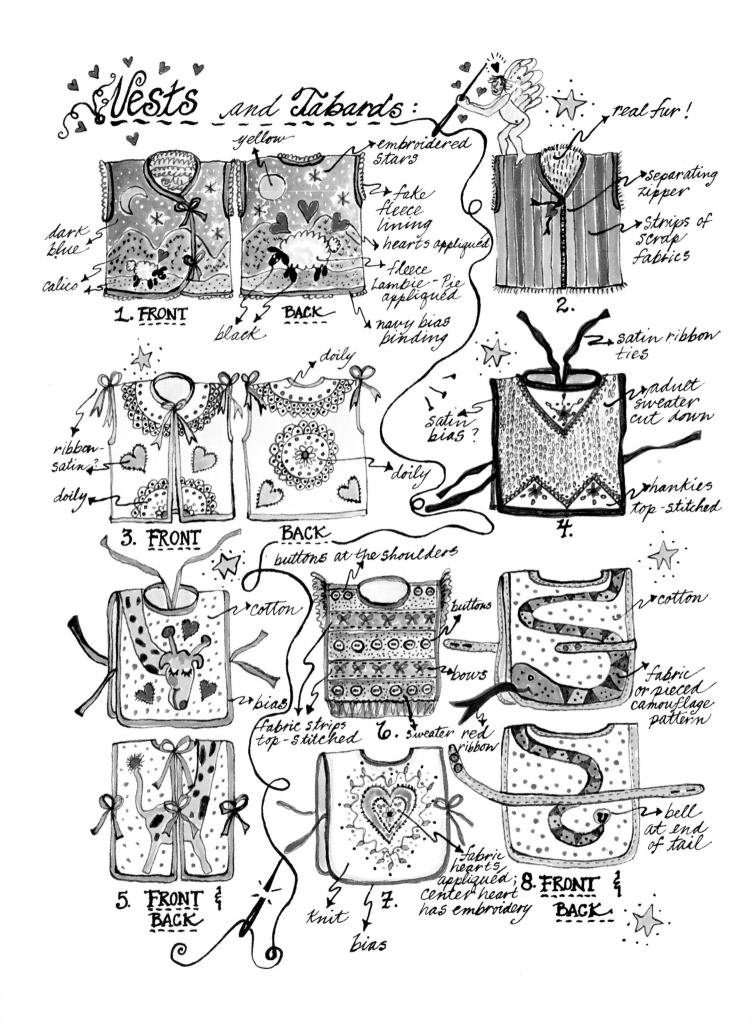

Nests and Tabards:

1. real fur!

yellow
embroidered stars
fake fleece lining
hearts appliquéd
fleece Lambie-Pie appliquéd
navy bias binding

dark blue
calico
black

1. FRONT   **BACK**

2.
separating zipper
strips of scrap fabrics

satin bias?

doily
ribbon-satin?
doily

3. FRONT   **BACK**

satin ribbon ties
adult sweater cut down
hankies top-stitched

4.

buttons at the shoulders
cotton
bias

buttons
bows

cotton

fabric strips top-stitched

6. sweater red ribbon

fabric or pieced camouflage pattern

fabric hearts appliquéd; center heart has embroidery

bell at end of tail

5. FRONT & BACK

7.
Knit
bias

8. FRONT & BACK

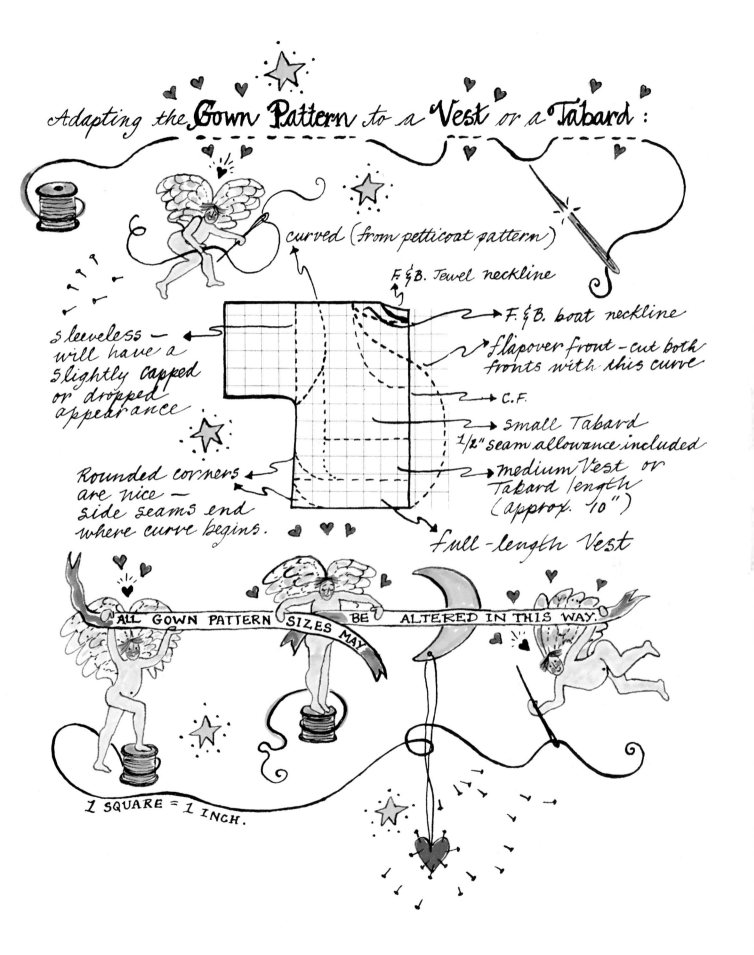

Adapting the **Gown Pattern** to a **Vest** or a **Tabard**:

curved (from petticoat pattern)

F. & B. Jewel neckline

F. & B. boat neckline

flapover front — cut both fronts with this curve

C.F.

small Tabard
1/2" seam allowance included

medium Vest or Tabard length (approx. 10")

full-length Vest

sleeveless —
will have a
slightly capped
or dropped
appearance

Rounded corners
are nice —
side seams end
where curve begins.

ALL GOWN PATTERN SIZES MAY BE ALTERED IN THIS WAY.

1 SQUARE = 1 INCH.

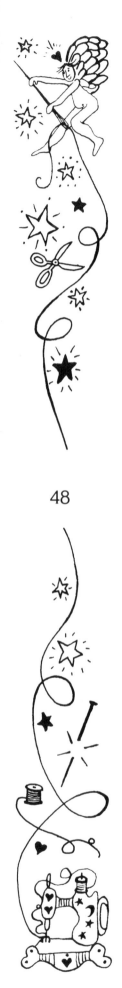

VESTS AND TABARDS

Vests and tabards are easily designed from Basic Pattern I.

For design inspiration look at the vests and tabards illustrated on page 46, then once again look around you for special textiles. These garments are so small that they make wonderful sampler projects: combinations of many needlework techniques and collages of found textiles can turn them into miniature works of art. And they are so versatile! They offer extra warmth in winter, and can be cool sunsuit tops in summer. Worn over a gown or jumpsuit, the vests or tabards create an outfit. Different vests paired with those two basic patterns can change the entire look from casual to dressy to a costume!

The vest illustrations include a landscape collage of printed wovens lined with a fake fleece to match the lamb in the collage; a collage of laces, embroideries, ribbons, and doilies; part of a special old sweater paired with stripes of woven fabrics and decorated with buttons and bows. And over the "alphabet" gown on page 20 is an ABC vest.

Fold over a large scarf or napkin, embroidered placemat, or lacy dresser scarf and practically all you have to do is to cut a neckline and you have a summer-weight tabard! Sandwich batting between two layers and it's warm enough for cool weather. Old sweaters are reused beautifully as tabards when the knit is bound with a contrasting woven binding. Or machine overcast and crochet the edges, or pick up stitches and do a few rows of knit ribbing (at the same gauge). Or you might cut a paper pattern, place it on a table or your lap, and use it as a guide to knit or crochet a tabard to the pattern dimensions. The rag-strip vest on pages 53-55 was done in this manner. This, then, can also become a background for even further embellishment.

The tabard, in particular, is a perfect backdrop for cheerful appliques. Many designs are offered throughout this book, and coloring books, magazines, puzzles, and children's books with simple illustrations also are good sources for applique outlines if you don't want to experiment with your own hand. Keep the outlines simple and you are virtually guaranteed successful design. For even more fun with baby, small washable doll "squeakers" (found in most craft supply stores) can be inserted under the applique before it is stitched down.

Before you begin your vest, make note of the following points:

1. Follow Basic Pattern I, pages 12-14. Use the straight dotted line cut-off (sleeveless) or the curved dotted line cut-off (petticoat) for armholes.

2. The vest can be any length you wish. Some of the vests look best at a length of approximately 10". Your baby's size will be the determining factor, as always.

3. If the vest or tabard is going to pull over the baby's head, and will not have closures at front, back, or shoulders, you will have to widen the neckline for an easy fit. The point at the shoulder where the dotted line of the petticoat neckline meets is a good point to extend the regular neckline. You may also want to scoop lower in the front and back to make a boat neckline.

4. For a deep front flap-over closure as in vest 1 on page 46, you will have to extend your pattern along the extension lines shown on the layout on page 47.

5. For added interest, consider curved ends on the side seams and on the ends of the front or back closing.

6. Unless you specifically desire the rounded jewel neckline of Basic Pattern I, the front, or lower, neckline should be used for both front and back pattern pieces.

7. If you plan to use a favorite old sweater or pair of socks for your vest or tabard, first determine whether you have sufficient fabric by laying the sweater or socks onto the paper pattern.

8. Tabards constructed of woven fabrics can provide extra warmth and will look very rich if they are quilted. Sandwich batting between two layers of fabric, then hand- or machine-quilt, even in a very simple pattern, as the last step before finishing the edges.

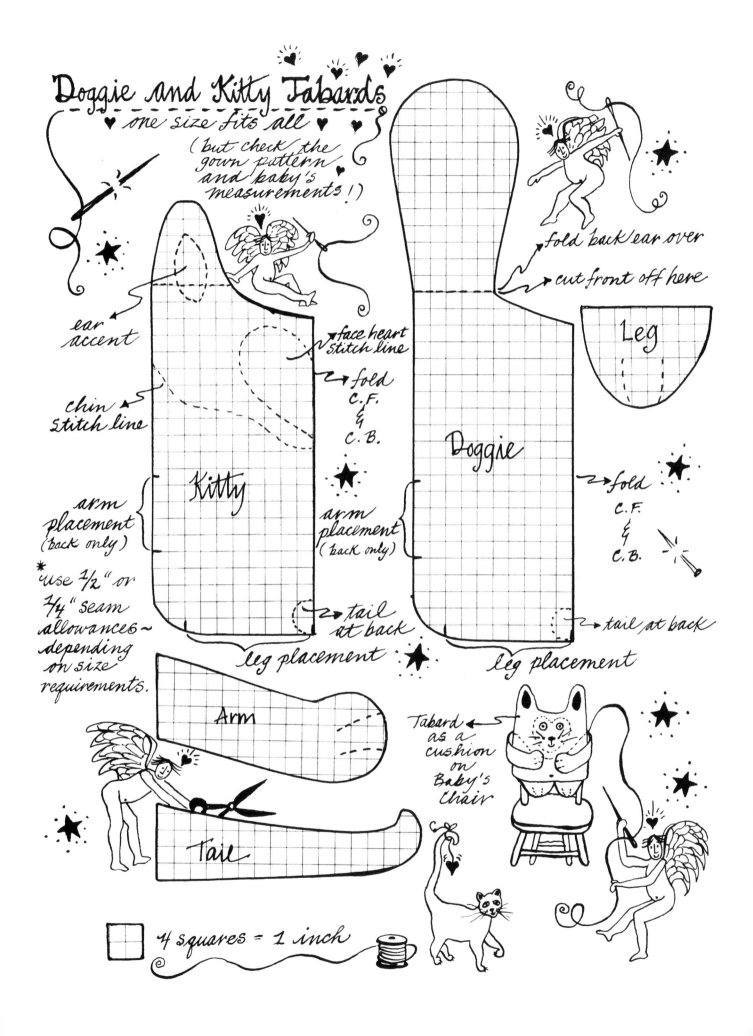

Doggie and Kitty Tabards

one size fits all

(but check the gown pattern and baby's measurements!)

ear accent

chin stitch line

Kitty

arm placement (back only)

*Use ½" or ¾" seam allowances ~ depending on size requirements.

face heart stitch line

fold C.F. & C.B.

arm placement (back only)

tail at back

leg placement

Arm

Tail

fold back ear over

cut front off here

Leg

Doggie

fold C.F. & C.B.

tail at back

leg placement

Tabard as a cushion on Baby's chair

4 squares = 1 inch

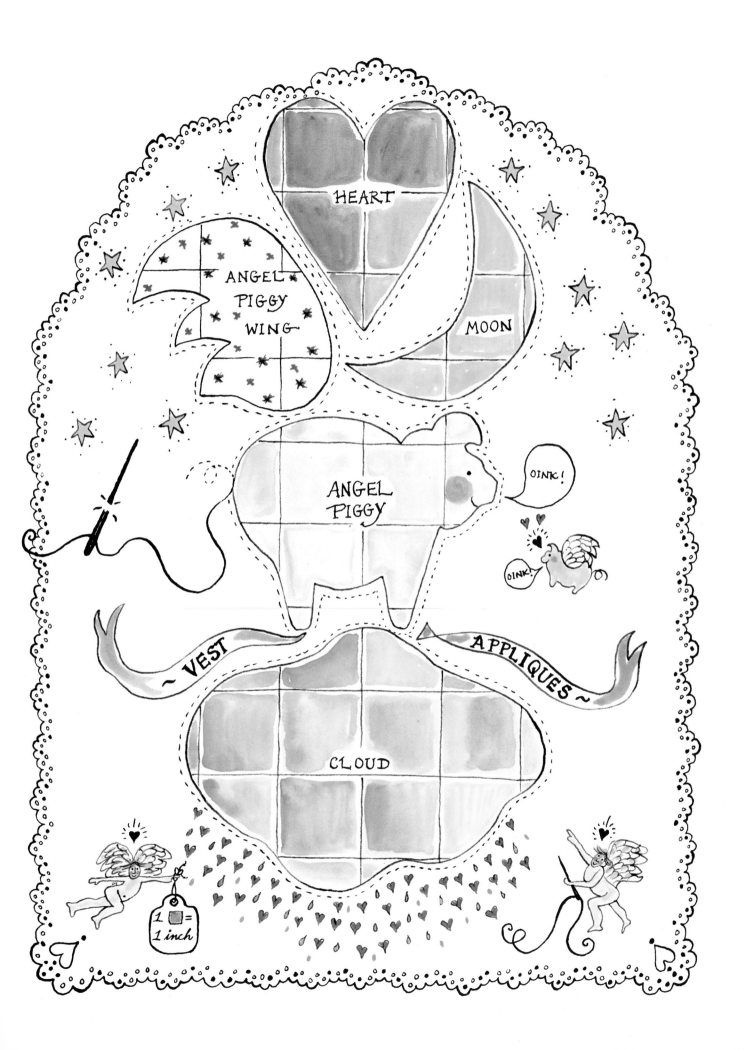

Angel Piggy Vest

An old, tattered, lightweight, handmade quilt was used for this vest. The top of the quilt had shredded beyond repair, as often happens when quilts are well used, but the underside showed row upon row of tiny, exquisite hand-stitching. Because it was white, it made a perfect background for the brightly colored appliques. It was lined with the same cotton print fabric as was used to make the gown shown with it on page 50.

If you do not have an old quilt at your disposal, you could use a lightweight mattress pad, quilted table protector, or a couple of quilted placemats. Or, if you have the time to spend, consider doing your own quilting, perhaps with white percale from old sheets or pillowcases.

The vest is made almost in the same way as the folk scarf vest (pages 15-18). Each front and back piece is attached to its lining piece then bound completely in bias tape. The lined pieces are then blind-stitched together at the shoulders and side seams. The gown shown with the vest has hearts along the bottom back, and a moon, hearts and a pig on the front hemline.

You will need:

- 1/3 yard each of quilted fabric and lining (calico?)
- scraps for appliques: blue, pink, red, yellow, and calico lining fabric
- 4 yellow star buttons · for vest back only, as these sometimes have sharp points and you don't want to have them in the front where baby can scratch herself
- yellow embroidery floss for stars on vest front
- blue embroidery floss for pigs' eyes
- pink embroidery floss for pigs' tails
- 1½ packages single-fold bias tape, green

Before you begin:

Check the Special Techniques section, page 101, for directions for the blind stitch and embroidery stitches: the "star," French knot, back stitch, and stem stitch.

Instructions:

1. Use the vest pattern layout on page 47.

2. Cut patterns with ¼" SA, as you are using a lining and a quilted fabric and all pieces will be completely bound with tape.

3. Cut out along the straight sleeveless line. Plan for a CF opening and round off CF corners at neckline and bottom corners.

4. Cut out appliques from scrap fabrics and pin them to the F and B of the quilt as in the illustration. Applique with a fine zigzag around each cut-out, using a corresponding color of thread.

5. With WST, baste lining to quilt at raw edges of front and back pieces.

6. Bind all around these three pieces with bias tape, being careful to hide the basting.

7. With the machine set to baste, quilt around the appliques with white thread.

8. Blind-stitch the shoulders and side seams together with bias tape, edges just touching.

9. Cut two 9" lengths of bias tape. Fold them lengthwise in half and stitch closed, turning in raw edges on the ends. Knot each end of the two pieces (ties), and secure one end to juncture of heart and cloud appliques at CF.

10. For each shoulder, make one bow of bias tape prepared in the same manner, and sew down firmly. These are optional and strictly decorative.

11. Sew star buttons onto the back.

12. Embroider yellow stars to the front; embroider pigs' eyes and tails in stem or back stitch.

52

Basic Pattern I:

Crocheted Rag Strip Vest

This is a long-range project. Do not consider crocheting the vest of rags if you are in a hurry. Choose, instead, to use ribbons, seam binding, or bias tape. All of these would be very expensive if purchased new because of the incredible amount of yardage needed, so look for scraps in thrift shops and beg for trimming scraps from friends. Thrift shops often have large spools of bias and ribbons which have been donated by industry. How lucky for you if you have come across such a treasure, because this is the perfect project in which to use trimmings.

If you have a sewing room filled with scraps, however, start making balls of rag strips. Make sure that the fabrics are all pre-washed to prevent shrinkage. Do not worry about raveled edges. As you crochet, some of them get turned in; the rest of the ragged edges add to the charm of the look. When you have a few balls, you can begin the actual crocheting, which in itself is an easy task. Tear washable cotton and cotton-blend fabrics into strips ¾" or 1" wide. Stitch the ends together to form a continuous "thread," and wind it into balls. You can have a color scheme, or you can use an "anything goes" approach. A multicolored vest uses up more scraps and will look smashing over any solid-color gown or jumpsuit.

You will need:

- size K crochet hook
- 4 very special buttons (we used pink bunnies)
- rag strip yardage of assorted prints and ribbons or seam binding

Instructions for estimating yardage:

1. See illustration of single crochet in the Special Techniques section. With size K crochet hook, chain 8 with a fairly loose tension, turn, skip 1 chain and single crochet (SC) 6 stitches (2 stitches should equal about 1"). Do a sample square of SC which should be approximately 3 x 3" with the same loose tension. Mark the end with a pin and unravel the sample. Measure the yardage you have used. You should have used approximately 4½ yards.

2. Cut a paper pattern, with no SA, for the vest you wish to crochet. Tape the pattern together as shown, and block it off into 3 x 3" squares. How many are there? Multiply this number by 4½ yards. How many yards do you need? Mind boggling, isn't it? Now you can understand why you might want to get your rag strips into large balls before even considering this project, as that is the most time-consuming part of it.

Instructions for rag strip vest:

1. Use a variation of the vest pattern on page 47.

2. Lay the paper pattern (without SA and taped at the shoulders) on a table.

3. Starting at the lower left corner of the back, work chain stitch to the lower right corner. Chain 2 for the turn.

4. Single crochet back and forth, to the point where the underarm curve begins. Then decrease at each side, following the pattern outline, until you reach the back neckline.

5. Now continue SC only on the right side and down the right front, decreasing as necessary to follow the front neckline and armhole curve of the paper pattern. Tie off when you have come to a front corner and when the SC work fits the pattern as closely as possible.

6. At the left back where you left off to complete the right front, tie on the rag stripping and repeat SC for the left front as you did for the right. Tie off.

7. Turn under all the hanging strips where you began or where you tied on and blind-stitch them to the inside of the vest so that they don't show.

8. Sew 4 buttons down the CF. To make corresponding buttonholes, simply pull an edge SC loop out to go around the buttons.

9. Sew side seams with a blind stitch.

53

Crocheted Rag Strip Vest:

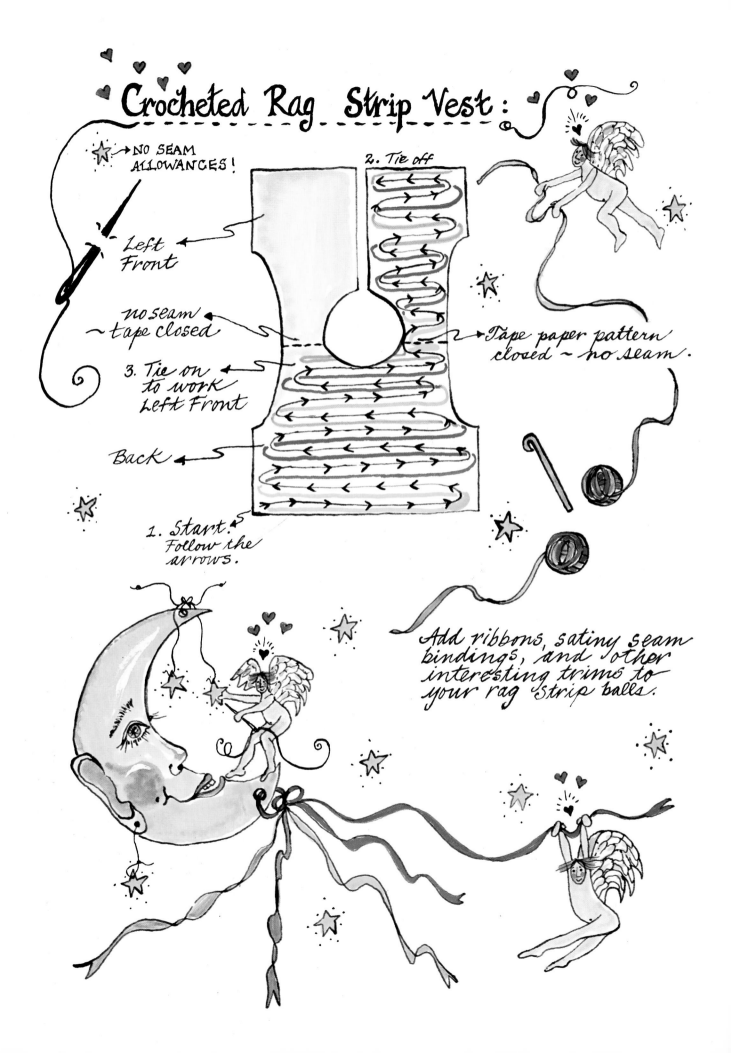

NO SEAM ALLOWANCES!

Left Front

no seam ~ tape closed

3. Tie on to work Left Front

Back

2. Tie off

Tape paper pattern closed ~ no seam.

1. Start. Follow the arrows.

Add ribbons, satiny seam bindings, and other interesting trims to your rag strip balls.

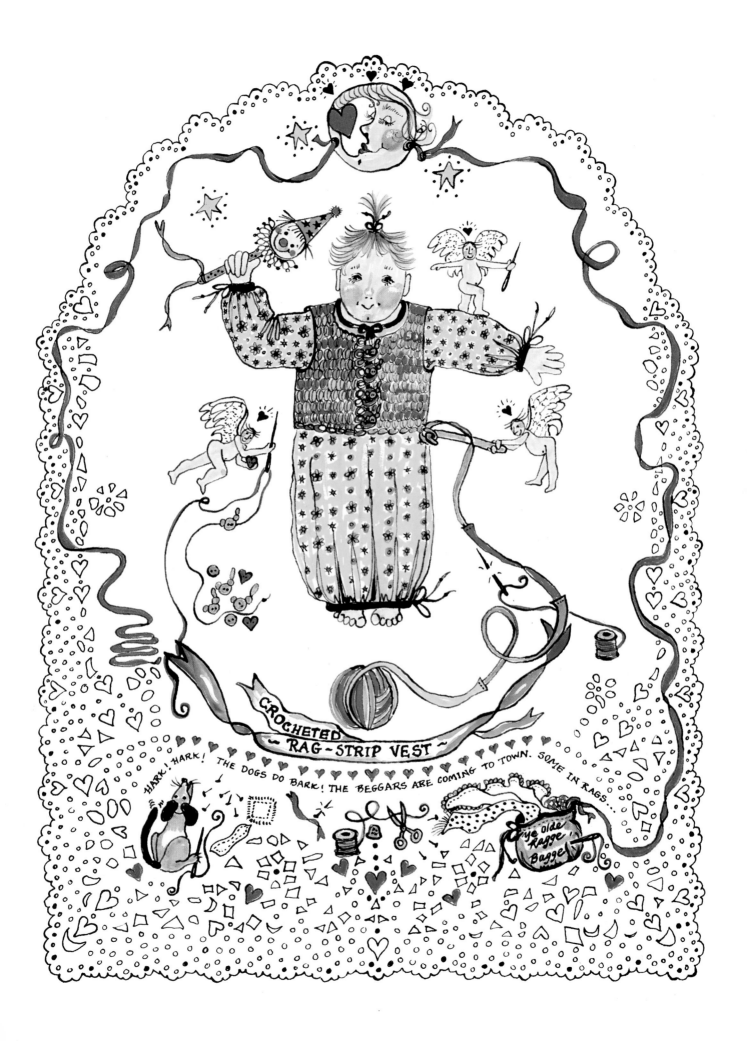

CROCHETED
~ RAG~STRIP VEST ~

HARK! HARK! THE DOGS DO BARK! THE BEGGARS ARE COMING TO TOWN. SOME IN RAGS...

ye olde Ragge Bagge

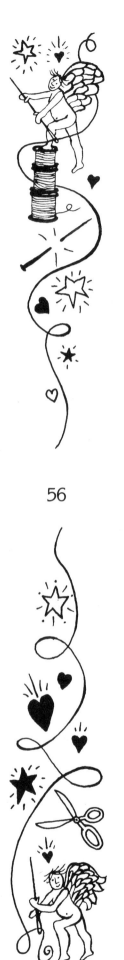

Basic Pattern II: JUMPSUIT AND VARIATIONS

If you draw an enlargement of one of the jumpsuit patterns and lay it over the gown pattern, Basic Pattern I, you will see that they are really the same. Only a crotch is added. However, for fewer lines and your ease in interpretation, the jumpsuit pattern is drawn for you here in the same three basic sizes.

The jumpsuits are roomy, as are the gowns, for two reasons. The first is baby's ease of movement. The second reason is that the crotch seam is a very simple one, with little curve, which means roominess must be achieved across the garment, as well as with a little extra length.

The variations illustrated are only a few, compared to the endless variety you will soon be thinking of! The jumpsuit can be cut long or short and with or without sleeves. It can open down the front or down the back, or the center front could be extended with a flap-over (as in the lamb vest on page 46). Since the patterns are all interchangeable, these digressions from the basic pattern are easy to achieve and are the goal of this book: to get **you** to be the designer!

With a waistline casing and a drawstring the jumpsuit has an entirely new look. Cut the pattern off just ¼" to ½" above the line for the waistline casing and you have pants, shorts, or overalls, depending upon your wish. Add a handkerchief, scarf, embroidered napkin, or quilted potholder for an eye-catching bib. The bib can be the background for your or your ancestors' needlework skills (some cross-stitch, a crocheted antimacassar?)

The shorter length pants (and sleeveless top portion) aren't limited to warm weather use. Imagine them in cold-weather fabrics over tights, shirts, and sweaters! In summer, old linen dresser scarves are just the right size for a short jumpsuit or sunsuit. Take another look at that new package of dishcloths you might have tucked away in a kitchen drawer. This is the perfect version of the jumpsuit in which to use a couple of them for an airy shirt and shorts.

Zippered fronts give a totally different, and more casual, look. Search for interesting old textile tidbits to make unusual zipper pulls (be sure they're soft). Or consider stitching and stuffing a small heart in one of the garment's fabrics to secure by a thread loop (see jumpsuit variation 2 on page 58).

Antimacassars, doilies, embroidered napkins, handkerchieves, and other fancy sturdy circles or squares work wonderfully as yoke accents over the shoulders or across the front and back. Use them cut in half and secured under bias tape for a stunning effect. A tabard can be used as a button-on or tie-on front and back yoke for the pants, too, as in the illustration on page 61.

56

Basic Pattern II.
Jumpsuits:

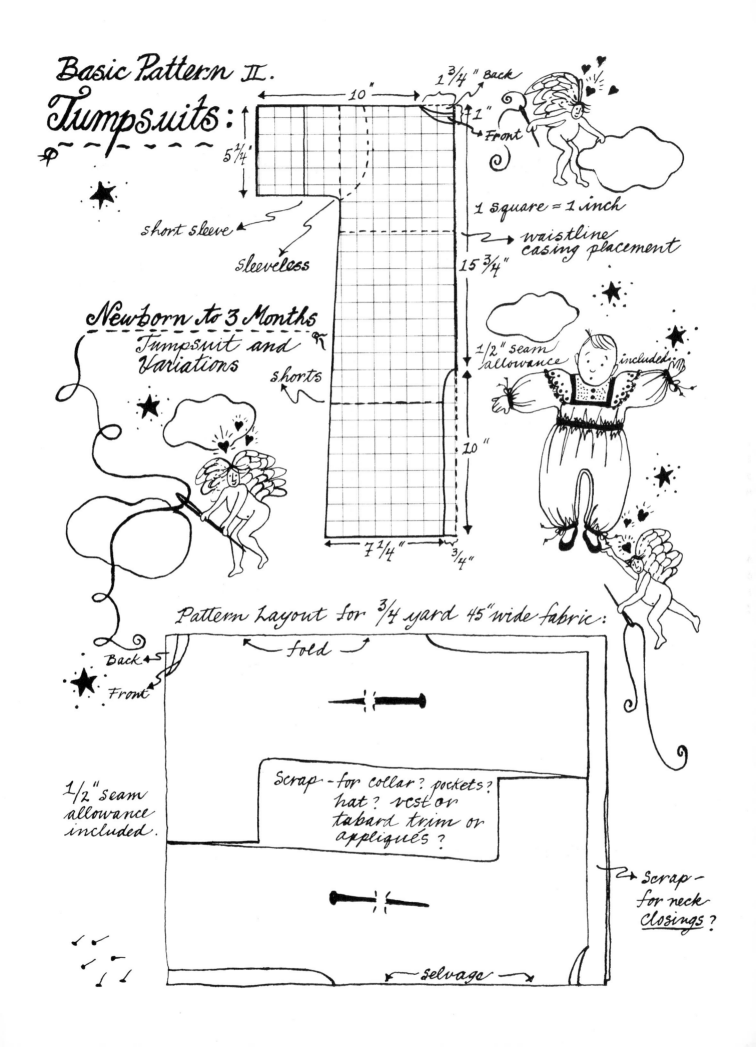

10"

1 3/4" Back

1"

Front

5 1/4"

short sleeve

sleeveless

1 square = 1 inch

waistline casing placement

15 3/4"

1/2" seam allowance — included

Newborn to 3 Months
Jumpsuit and Variations

shorts

7 1/4"

3/4"

10"

Pattern Layout for 3/4 yard 45" wide fabric:

fold

Back

Front

1/2" seam allowance included.

Scrap — for collar? pockets? hat? vest or tabard trim or appliqués?

Scrap — for neck closings?

selvage

Jumpsuits, Pants, Overalls, Shorts:

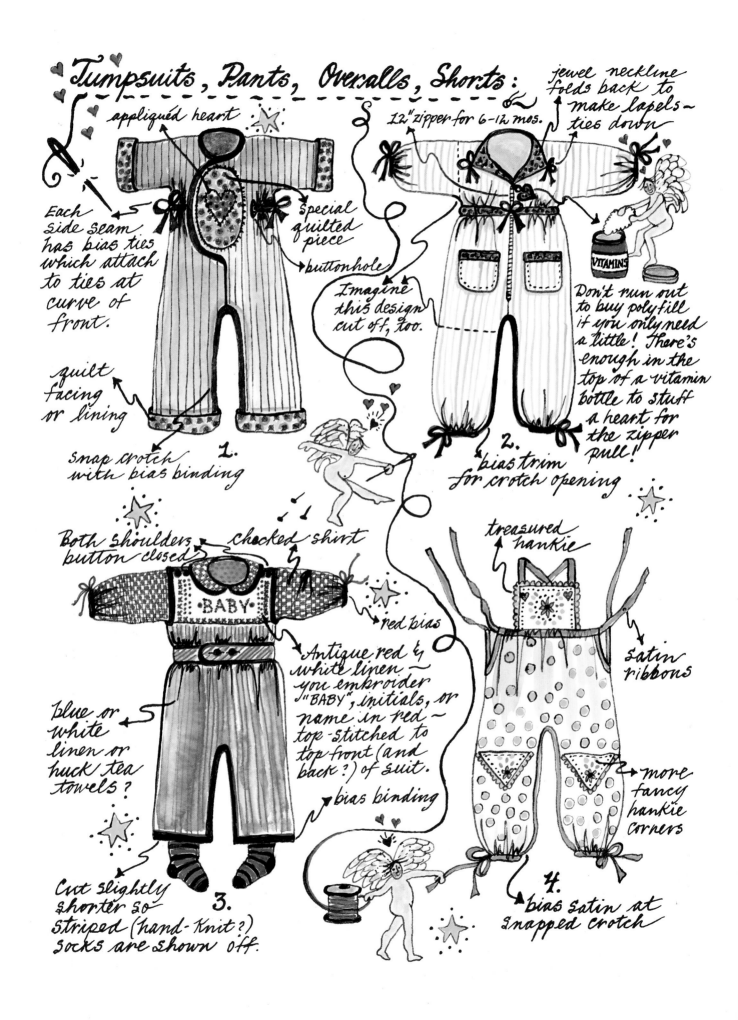

appliquéd heart

special quilted piece

buttonhole

Each side seam has bias ties which attach to ties at curve of front.

quilt facing or lining

snap crotch with bias binding

1.

Imagine this design cut off, too.

12" zipper for 6-12 mos.

jewel neckline folds back to make lapels~ ties down

VITAMINS

Don't run out to buy polyfill if you only need a little! There's enough in the top of a vitamin bottle to stuff a heart for the zipper pull!

2.

bias trim for crotch opening

Both shoulders button closed

checked shirt

BABY

Blue or white linen or huck tea towels?

Cut slightly shorter so striped (hand-knit?) socks are shown off.

3.

red bias

Antique red & white linen ~ you embroider "BABY", initials, or name in red ~ top-stitched to top front (and back?) of suit.

bias binding

treasured hankie

satin ribbons

more fancy hankie corners

4.

bias satin at snapped crotch

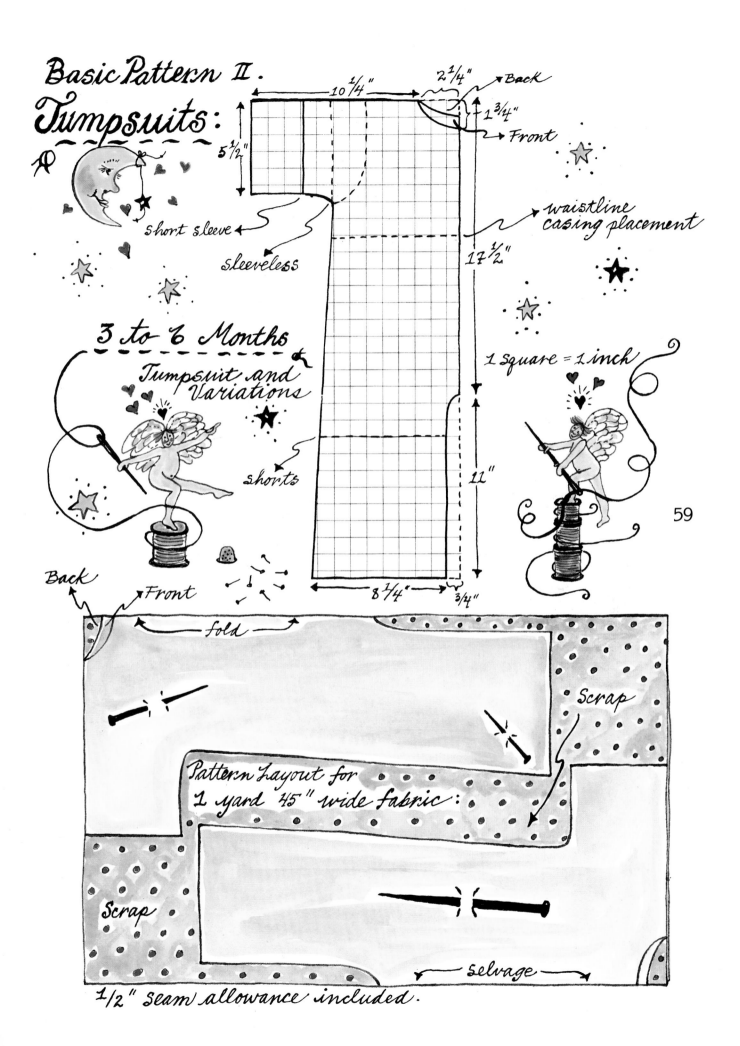

Basic Pattern II.
Jumpsuits:

10 1/4"

2 1/4" → Back

5 1/2"

1 3/4"

→ Front

short sleeve ←

sleeveless

waistline
casing placement

17 1/2"

3 to 6 Months
Jumpsuit and Variations

1 square = 1 inch

shorts

11"

59

8 1/4"   3/4"

Back

Front

fold

Scrap

Pattern Layout for
1 yard 45" wide fabric:

Scrap

selvage

1/2" seam allowance included.

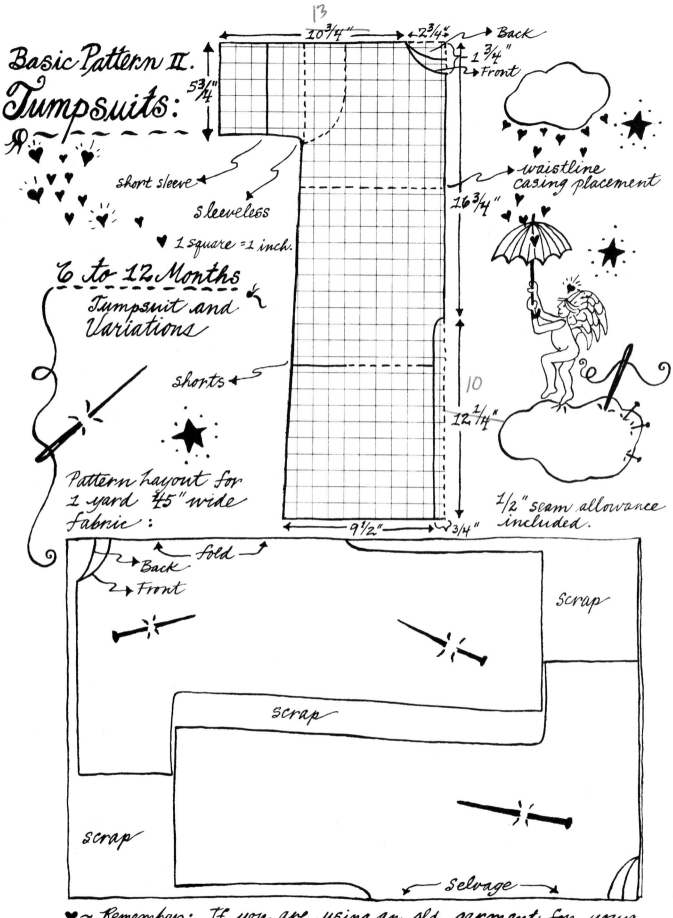

Basic Pattern II.
Jumpsuits:

5¾"

13

10¾"

2¾"

Back

1¾"
Front

short sleeve

sleeveless

♥ 1 square = 1 inch.

waistline
casing placement

16¾"

6 to 12 Months
Jumpsuit and
Variations

shorts

10

12¼"

Pattern layout for
1 yard 45" wide
fabric:

9½"

¾"

½" seam allowance
included.

Back
fold
Front

scrap

scrap

scrap

scrap

selvage

♥ ~ Remember: If you are using an old garment for your
jumpsuit, the sleeves can be attached separately by
cutting the pattern off at the straight sleeveless line.

Jumpsuits for Warm Weather:

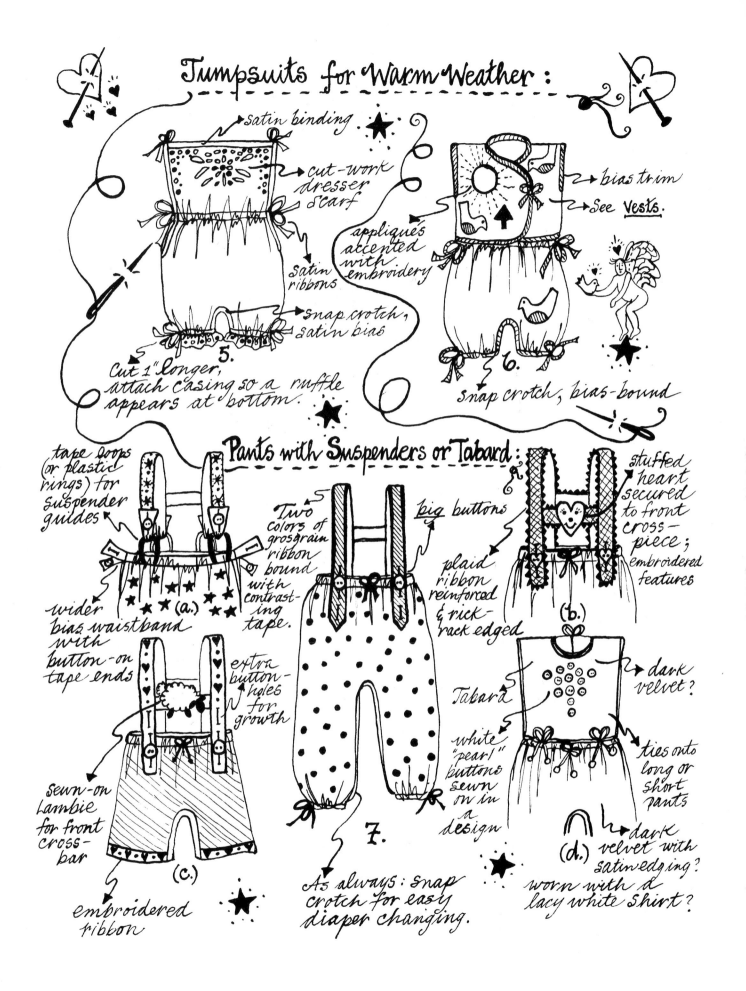

satin binding

cut-work dresser scarf

appliqués accented with embroidery

satin ribbons

snap crotch, satin bias

bias trim

See Vests.

5.

Cut 1" longer, attach casing so a ruffle appears at bottom.

6.

snap crotch, bias-bound

Pants with Suspenders or Tabard:

tape loops (or plastic rings) for suspender guides

wider bias waistband with button-on tape ends

sewn-on Lambie for front cross-bar

embroidered ribbon

(a.)

(c.)

Two colors of grosgrain ribbon bound with contrasting tape.

big buttons

plaid ribbon reinforced & rick-rack edged

extra button-holes for growth

7.

As always: snap crotch for easy diaper changing.

stuffed heart secured to front cross-piece; embroidered features

(b.)

Tabard

white "pearl" buttons sewn on in a design

dark velvet?

ties onto long or short pants

(d.) dark velvet with satin edging? worn with a lacy white shirt?

~ CLASSIC ROMPER SUIT ~

UNDER THE SUN
THERE'S NOTHING NEW;
POEM OR PUN, UNDER THE SUN,
SAID SOLOMON,
AND HE SAID IT TRUE.
UNDER THE SUN
THERE'S NOTHING NEW.

~ Henry Charles Beeching ~

LET'S **ALL** GO OUT
AND SIT UNDER
THE **MOON** !

Basic Pattern II:
Classic Romper Suit

Old photographs dating from the 1930's back to the late 1800's, and paintings from even earlier times, picture baby boys in exquisite short-legged, one-piece suits. The fronts were often tucked, the waists loosely gathered with two-button fabric belts, and the necks accented with beautiful white lace or lace-edged white linen collars. Special fabrics like velvet, velveteen, or soft woolen blends were used then, and today flannel would be a nice addition to the list as it takes on an elegant look when dressed up with lace and fancy buttons. For summer wear, the suits were made in cotton and sometimes soft linen. Almost any fabric choice, though, would work for this timeless design. Just keep in mind how much time you are willing to spend on care when selecting your fabric.

The basic jumpsuit pattern makes the project an easy one to construct with either a front or back neck opening, depending where you place your center front and/or center back lines.

You will need:
- 3/4 yard fabric of your choice
- For collar: 1/3 yard white fabric, 1/3 yard iron-on interfacing, 1 yard narrow lace for trim

  or

  ready-made lace collar or antique collar
- 1/3 yard white fabric for cuffs (optional)
- 2 packages single-fold bias tape (cotton or rayon depending on fabric used for suit)
- 1/2 yard satin ribbon 1" to 1½" wide, for neckline bow
- 4 or 5 buttons for back neck opening
- 7 decorative buttons—3 for center front, 2 for each arm cuff, 2 for each leg cuff (optional)
- 7 to 9 size 1 sew-on snaps for crotch opening

63

Before you begin:
Refer to the Special Techniques section (page 101) for information on seam finishes, applying collars, finishing hems, neckline openings, and mock tatting.

Instructions:
1. Use Basic Pattern II, pages 57-60.

2. If you use velvet, velveteen, corduroy or other napped fabrics, be sure to lay pattern onto fabric with all pieces going in the same direction.

3. Add 1½" at CF for three ¼" tucks at either side of the CF. Mark the tucks as follows: measure ½" in from each side of the CF for the first tucks (¼" each); then ¼" away from the first, mark the second ¼" tucks; and ¼" away from the second, tucks, mark the third set.

4. Hand- or machine-stitch the tucks, making sure both the top (neckline) and bottom stitches are very secure. Press each set of tucks away from CF.

5. Determine where you would like the belt to be, and mark each side seam for loops. Mark halfway between the side seams and the center front on each side of the center front for two more belt loops in front and two in back.

6. Using ½" SA and the seam finish of your choice, sew shoulder seams and side seams closed. Press.

7. Finish the crotch opening. Wait to sew on the snaps after garment is completed.

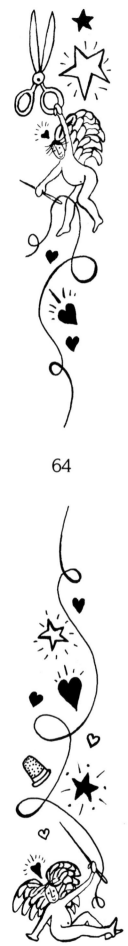

8. To finish arm and leg openings, sew single-fold bias tape to the arms and leg openings with RST, using ¼" SA. Turn, press, and blind-stitch the bias to wrong sides of sleeves. Press. Or finish with cuffs:

Measure circumference of arm and leg openings and add 1" (½" SA for each end). Cut two pieces of white fabric this length for each arm and each leg (eight pieces, or two sets for each arm and each leg). Make the height (width) of the cuffs about 1½".

If you are using lightweight cuff fabric, cut two cuffs of identical size from iron-on inter-facing, and apply it before proceeding.

With RST and ½" SA, sew each set of cuffs along the length. Trim SA to ¼" and press open. Do not make this "circlet" for the legs because of the snap crotch.

Lining up the romper underarm seams with the cuffs' width seams, pin right sides of cuffs to wrong sides of armholes. Sew ½" SA, trim, and press SA down into cuffs.

Fold cuffs up along the lengthwise seamlines, turn, and press raw edges under ½" (at this point you can insert lace before you pin cuff to outside of sleeve) and pin to outside of the sleeves. Blind-stitch cuffs in place, catching the lace in as you sew.

On the legs, turn the width (height) raw edges ½" to the inside and press. Lining up these folded edges with the finished crotch-end edges, pin the right sides of cuffs to wrong sides of leg openings. Machine-stitch with ½" SA. Trim SA and press down into the cuffs.

Finish leg cuffs as you did the sleeve cuffs.

9. Finish back neck opening.

10. To construct a belt:

Determine belt length: measure around waistline of the garment; add 5" (2" overlap on each end for buttons and buttonholes plus ½" SA for each end). Cut two pieces of romper fabric at this length and 2½" wide. If the fabric is lightweight, cut one piece of iron-on interfacing of the same measurements and apply it to the wrong side of one belt piece.

With RST and using ½" SA, sew belt together around two long sides and across one end. Leave one end open to turn the belt to right side. Trim SA to ¼", turn, and press. Turn the open end ½" to the inside and blind-stitch closed. Press. The belt can, at this point, be top-stitched ¼" from the edges all around for added firmness and/or decoration.

Determine how tight you wish the belt to be worn around baby's waist and place two buttonholes at one end, approximately 1" apart. Sew on corresponding buttons.

11. Work thread-loop carriers of mock tatting to correspond with the width of the belt at the markings you made at the side seams, front, and back.

12. Sew on the crotch snaps.

13. Sew decorative buttons to CF and sides of the arm and leg cuffs.

14. Tack the ribbon at the CF of collar. Tie it into a loopy bow. Hem the ends or cut them on a decorative slant.

64

Basic Pattern II:

Doily-Shouldered Suit

Before you begin, read over the following directions in the Special Techniques section (page 101): French seam, crotch finish, sleeve and leg finish, neckline finish, embroidery stitches.

You will need:

- 1 yard woven fabric 45" wide (cotton blend calico or a recycled garment of your choice)
- 2 packages single-fold bias tape (we chose bright pink and a rusty red to correspond with the pink and red in our calico print)
- 1 doily or antimacassar approximately 9 or 10" square, or can be greater in length, but not wider than 10"
- embroidery floss in assorted colors
- 3 baby buttons
- 3 or 4 size 3/0 sew-on snaps, for back opening
- 9 size 1 sew-on snaps, for crotch opening

Instructions:

1. Use Basic Pattern II, pages 57-60.

2. Enlarge and cut the pattern to your own specifications, using long sleeves, long legs, and a back neck opening. Mark fabric for waistline casing placement.

3. Sew shoulder-to-sleeve seams closed with French seams. Press.

4. Mark CF with a pin. Sew two tucks, each 1¾" long by 3/16" wide, ⅜" to the right and the left of CF. Press tucks to outside.

5. Cut doily or antimacassar in half along width dimension. Mark center and pin each half over shoulder seam approximately 1" in from neckline, with centers on shoulder seams.

6. Cut a length of bias tape 5¼" long. Center it across CF and tucks, 1½" down from CF neckline. Top-stitch it across as shown in illustration on next page.

7. Cut two lengths of bias tape the same measurement as raw edge of doily, plus ½" (for a ¼" turn-under of raw edge at each end).

8. Pin these bias lengths ⅛" over raw edge of antimacassar, catching ⅛" of each raw edge of the pink bias cross-piece as you do so. Top-stitch down. Press.

9. Sew side seams closed with French seams. Sew CB seam closed 4½" to 5" up from crotch with a regular seam, then zigzag edges to overcast them.

10. Finish CB with bias tape. Finish sleeve ends, crotch, and leg ends as instructed in Special Techniques section.

11. Top-stitch bias tape along waistline marking, turning end raw edges in ½" to 1" at edge of CB bias tape edging, and leaving open there for drawstring to be shirred through.

12. For waist drawstring, cut a 36 to 38" length of bias and sew closed lengthwise. Shirr it through the openings left at the casing ends. Knot the ends of the drawstrings.

13. Finish neckline with bias tape.

14. Sew 3 tiny buttons down CF between tucks. Sew 3 snaps down CB. Sew 9 snaps along crotch opening.

15. Embroider flowers, leaves, and French knots in the sections blocked off by bias in the front.

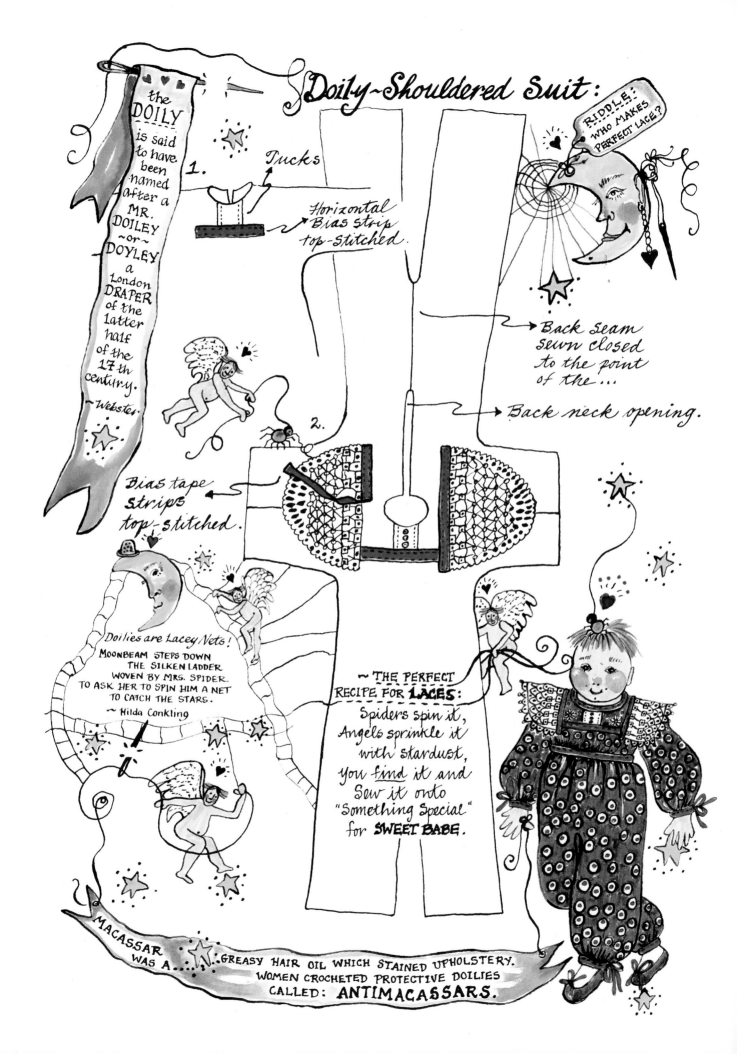

Doily-Shouldered Suit:

the DOILY is said to have been named after a **MR. DOILEY** ~or~ **DOYLEY** a London **DRAPER** of the latter half of the 17th century. ~Webster

1.

Tucks

Horizontal Bias strip top-stitched.

RIDDLE: WHO MAKES PERFECT LACE?

Back Seam sewn closed to the point of the...

Back neck opening.

Bias tape **strips** top-stitched.

2.

Doilies are Lacey Nets!
MOONBEAM STEPS DOWN THE SILKEN LADDER WOVEN BY MRS. SPIDER TO ASK HER TO SPIN HIM A NET TO CATCH THE STARS.
~ Hilda Conkling

~ THE PERFECT RECIPE FOR **LACES**:
Spiders spin it, Angels sprinkle it with stardust, you <u>find</u> it and Sew it onto "Something Special" for **SWEET BABE**.

MACASSAR WAS A...... GREASY HAIR OIL WHICH STAINED UPHOLSTERY. WOMEN CROCHETED PROTECTIVE DOILIES CALLED: **ANTIMACASSARS.**

RECYCLING KNITS

As you have undoubtedly ascertained by now, one of the main purposes of this book is to encourage the experienced needlecrafter to try to see things in new ways; in particular to find new and imaginative uses for deserving textiles. This goal is especially easy to achieve when you consider knit garments.

Old sweaters and knit shirts can be re-used in exciting ways to clothe a baby. Sweater sleeves are perfect legs for jumpsuits and drawstring pants. If the sweater has worn elbows, cut the sleeves off just below the holes to make two legs. They can be combined with other yarns, with other knits, or with woven fabrics to make a very special pair of pants.

If you are fortunate enough to have an old raglan-sleeved sweater, you can use the top portions of the raglans as front and back bibs for a pair of overalls. (In fact, sleeves of any fabric can be used this way.) Cuffs that are too large can be shirred to the size of the baby's ankle with a drawstring.

Adults' knit ski caps, when cut into two square or rectangular pieces, are the beginnings of a tabard or vest—the foundation work is done for you! By crocheting or knitting any necessary additions in contrasting or coordinating yarns, appliquing special features, or embroidering your own touches, you can quickly complete a rewarding project.

A special outgrown or outdated hand-knit sweater can be turned into a bunting, long jumper, or little dress. If the wool is too scratchy, line the new garment with a smooth, light-weight fabric.

Knit scarves and mufflers offer unlimited possibilities for baby clothing, and can become sweaters, tabards, or overall bibs. If you have several scarves which look good together, you can hand-stitch them to make a crazy quilt knit blanket. The yarns you use to sew the scarves together will be important, as the color or hue will affect the finished product's appeal. Light-weight knit mittens and gloves can be shaped into charming appliques to sew to the knit blanket. Worn or stained areas can be embroidered over with colorful crewel yarns.

There are two different ways to incorporate an old knit garment into a new baby garment. One involves combining the knit garment parts with some woven fabric. The only real trick is to make sure that the knit pieces you are going to sew into woven fabric areas do not stretch too much to fit smoothly. To prevent stretching, overcast the cut edge of the knit with a wide zigzag stitch, then steam it until it is the proper size. Then use a zigzag stitch to join the knit to the woven fabric. If you are going to put a woven binding onto a knit fabric, a straight stitch can be used and should work accurately if you pin often.

The other way to use an old knit for a new garment is to cut, then unravel the knit piece until it is the size you need for the project. Choose a knitting needle (or crochet hook) that will give you same gauge, pick up the loops on the needles and form the garment to your design specifications by adding your own knitting to it. This works particularly well when you are making pant legs from sweater sleeves. Or, all cut edges of the knit piece can be overcast with machine zigzag then bound with an edging of single crochet. The front loops of the single crochet stitches can then be picked up on knitting needles, or additional crochet can be worked.

Beautiful socks need not be discarded when holes appear in heels or toes. There is a surprising amount of fabric in a sock! The argyle pullover on page 71 demonstrates how nicely you will be able to work an old pair of socks into a wonderful sweater for baby. A simpler way to use the sock would be to make it into a snuggly tabard.

A warm baby bonnet can be fashioned from a pair of old sock tops. By cutting off the foot at the heel then slitting each tube open at a logical point in the pattern, the two can be joined together to make one large tube. If baby's head is too large for this design, edgings of knit or crochet can be added to the sides to expand them before joining. The top raw edge can be gathered closed and pom-pommed. Crocheted, braided, or Scandinavian twisted ties can be used under the chin. If there is enough knit fabric in the instep of the sock and it is free of damage, two little ear flaps can be fashioned and sewn to the sides of the cap before the chin ties are attached.

Now it is your turn to think up your own answers to the riddle "When is a sock not a sock?".

67

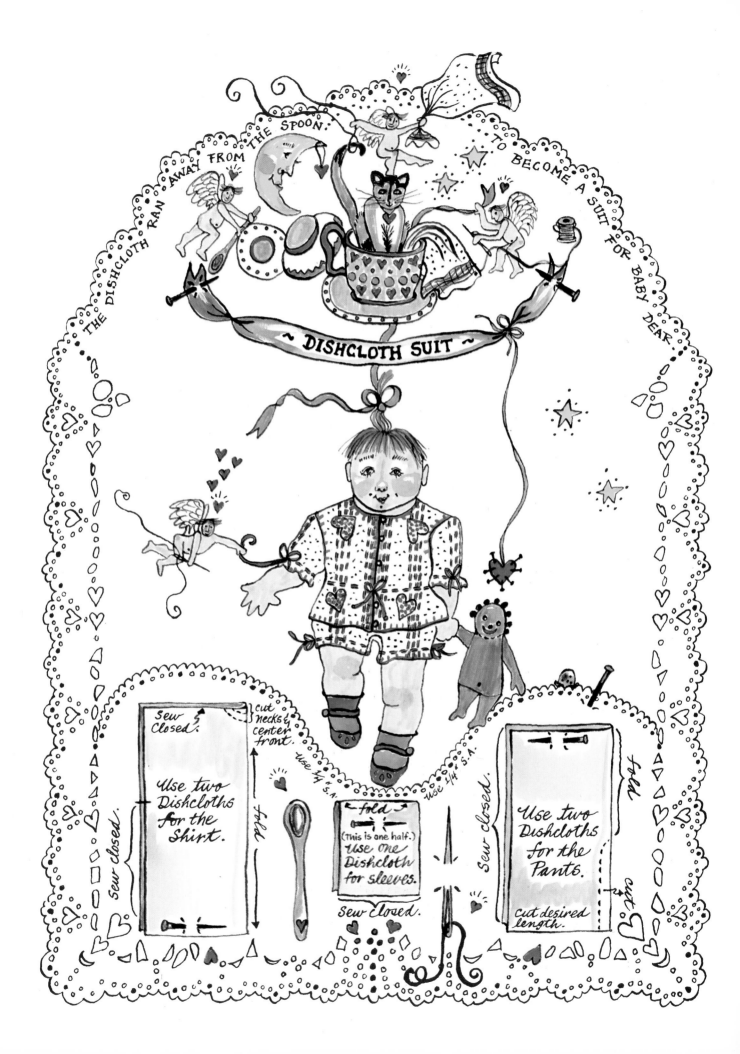

THE DISHCLOTH RAN AWAY FROM THE SPOON. TO BECOME A SUIT FOR BABY DEAR.

~ DISHCLOTH SUIT ~

Sew Closed.

cut necks & center front.

Use two Dishcloths for the Shirt.

Sew closed.

fold

Use 1/4 S.A.

fold
(This is one half.)
Use one Dishcloth for sleeves.

Sew closed.

Use 1/4 S.A.

Sew closed.

Use two Dishcloths for the Pants.

fold

cut

cut desired length.

Basic Pattern ll:
Dishcloth Suit

Every now and then a garment design idea comes along for which nothing will work as well as a brand new textile. This project is one where the use of a time-worn fabric will not add charm—but there probably aren't many who would consider using an old dishrag to clothe a child!

New dishcloths made of 100% cotton mesh can be found in brilliant color combinations. Because of their airy, open-weave construction, dishcloths make wonderfully cool baby clothing for warm weather. Cotton dishcloths are manufactured in many grades (weights and quality of construction). For the suit illustrated here, we used a dishcloth with an off-white background and blue, red, and green threads running through. The package was labeled "utility" or "heavy-duty." The cloths are woven cotton, but because of the very loose weave, the project is approached as if they were knits. The heart applique accents are woven calico in red, blue, and green.

This type of cloth washes beautifully, holds up well, and softens with wear. Before beginning the project, wash the cloths in hot water and tumble dry to achieve maximum shrinkage. Some packages give the cloth dimensions, which should be helpful to you, but many do not. So if you buy, say, 13" by 17" cloths, you might expect them to shrink to about 12" by 14". You might find that a 13" by 13" cloth shrinks very little. You will really have to experiment and be prepared to piece on more dishcloth in spots.

If the dishcloths are just not large enough for your pattern size, there are two alternative approaches you might consider: you can buy an extra package of cloths and piece them as necessary with single crochet, which also is used to assemble the garment, or you can add extra rows of single crochet to the edges which later will be finished in that manner.

You will need:
- 2 to 3 packages of "utility" or "heavy-duty" 100% cotton dishcloths (You can always use extras to—ugh!—wash dishes!)
- acrylic yarns—blue and red sport weight or colors to coordinate with your cloths
- crochet hook size G
- 6 wonderful buttons (approximately ⅜") for jacket front
- large-eyed tapestry needle
- 7 size 1 sew-on snaps for crotch opening

Before you begin:
Read in the Special Techniques section (page 101) about finishing the raw edges of knits, French knots, single crochet, Scandinavian twisted ties, braided yarn ties.

Instructions for shirt:

1. After pre-shrinking the dishcloths, place them **on top** of the basic jumpsuit paper pattern (pages 57-60) to cut the neckline and sleeve openings.

2. Fold each dishcloth in half (lengthwise, if the cloths are not perfectly square). The fold lines go on the CF and CB lines. The top selvage edges of the dishcloth should be placed ¼" below the shoulder of the pattern front and back to compensate for less than ½" SA. You will simply be overcasting the seam edges at about ¼" from the edges.

3. The sleeves are made from one dishcloth cut in half. Zigzag the cut edges with RST to form a tube.

4. Pin cloth onto paper pattern. Flip it over and cut away the dishcloth at the front and back necklines. Mark point of the underarm on both pieces. Cut open CF (fold). Remove fabric from paper pattern.

5. Finish all cut edges with machine zigzag stitch and steam press, if necessary, to prevent stretching.

6. Pin heart appliques onto front and back of shirt in any way which pleases you, or as the design illustrates. Machine-applique twice around the hearts: the first time with a wide zigzag basting stitch (to prevent too much stretching), and the second time with a zigzag applique stitch. Steam press.

7. With RST, zigzag overcast the shoulders very close to the edges. Turn to right side.

8. Embellish the lines of colored threads with your own embroidery stitches (French knots add textural interest).

9. With blue yarn, single crochet an edging around neckline, CF, bottom and sleeve openings, then around both ends of sleeves.

10. Hand-stitch sleeves to sleeve openings with blue yarn.

11. With red yarn, make Scandinavian twisted or braided yarn ties. Use them to gather the sleeves to puff, and tie in bows. A large tapestry needle works well for this. Gather the waist slightly in the same manner, leaving the ends long enough to tie at the waist. Knot yarn ends.

12. Sew buttons onto one center front edge. One yarn of the single crochet on the opposite center front edge can then be gently pulled over each button as a buttonhole.

Instructions for pants:

1. Use two dishcloths for the pants, folding them in half for the CF and CB. Use the same options for enlarging the dishcloths, if necessary.

2. Cut the crotch openings and zigzag the raw edges.

3. Finish leg bottoms, crotch openings, and around the waist with single crochet worked in blue yarn.

4. Accentuate color lines of dishcloth with French knots of red yarn as on shirt.

5. Make ties to gather the waistline and the legs. Use two ties for each leg; the ends will be secured at the crotch opening before threading each toward the center side where they will meet and tie.

6. Sew snaps onto crotch opening.

Pullover from Argyle Socks

Years ago, darning socks was an endless, routine household chore. Socks were hand-knit, so a worn one was rarely discarded until it no longer warranted the time needed to mend it, then the yarns would usually be unravelled and saved for another purpose.

Today, few of us take the time to mend heels and toes, and worn socks are just thrown out. Reconsider! You will be amazed at the amount of knit fabric a sock yields when it is cut open and laid flat. Sweet little sweaters for newborns can be made from them with the addition of some single crochet and a few basic knitting stitches.

Of course not all socks are worth using for this purpose. Be discriminating, because this project requires a significant amount of time. Argyle and other patterned knits are very good choices. You may even be fortunate enough to find an old pair of hand-knit socks.

Analyze the fiber content of the socks you plan to use, and purchase color-coordinated yarn of the same kind. If the socks are machine knit, the gauge will be very fine. Do not try to duplicate it. A three-ply sport weight or four-ply yarn will work very nicely with a size 00 crochet hook and numbers 3 and 5 knitting needles.

The argyle socks we used for the illustrated sweater are acrylic, in navy blue, brick red, hunter green, and oatmeal. Both shoulders unbutton for ease in pulling over baby's head.

Instructions that follow are for a sweater sized for a newborn to three-month-old baby. For the larger sizes you will need more socks, but several different patterns can be used together very successfully with the right yarns to join them. Use Basic Pattern I, page 12, for general shape and size.

You will need:

- 1 pair patterned ladies' knee socks or men's regular length socks
- less than 1 skein each of 4-ply knitting yarn in 3 colors to coordinate with your socks (we used navy, brick red, and oatmeal)
- 6 buttons (about ½" diameter) for shoulders
- size 00 crochet hook
- knitting needles, sizes 3 and 5
- tapestry or other large-eyed needle for assembly

71

Before you begin:

Refer to the Special Techniques section, beginning on page 101, for knit and crochet stitch instructions.

If you plan to follow the knitting instructions given here, do a gauge swatch. Working in pattern with 4-ply yarn and numbers 3 and 5 needles: 5 sts = 1 inch; 6 rows = 1 inch.

Prepare the socks:

1. Cut off foot portion of each sock just above the heel.

2. On each sock, measure 5 to 5½" down from top. Cut off at the pattern completion closest to that measurement. These two tubes will become the sweater sleeves.

3. Slit the remaining two tubes vertically, between pattern repeats if possible. You now have two rectangles, each approximately 5½" high by 6½" wide, for the sweater front and back.

4. Overcast all cut edges with a zigzag basting stitch. Steam press to regain an approximation of the original dimensions.

Instructions for sweater:

1. At the top and bottom edges of each rectangle, crochet an edging of 24 evenly spaced stitches in SC using navy or red yarn. Set one piece aside for the sweater back.

2. With red yarn, work a row of SC around the ribbed edges of the tubes that will be the sleeves. With navy yarn, work a row of SC around the machine-finished raw edge of each.

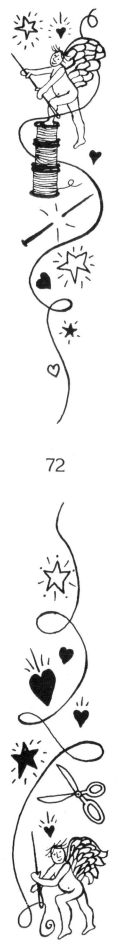

Front:

1. With number 5 needles, pick up front loop of each stitch of crocheted edging at top of the argyle rectangle (24 stitches).

2. Tie on oatmeal yarn, and on RS of rectangle, work simple checkerboard stitch for 12 rows (twelfth row will be on WS).

3. On RS and continuing with checkerboard stitch, work 6 sts. Place the 18 remaining sts onto stitch holder. Continue working checkerboard stitch on 6 remaining sts for 9 more rows to complete left center front portion of sweater. Bind off in checkerboard stitch.

4. Tie on oatmeal yarn and work checkerboard stitch across the 12 center sts. Place them on a stitch holder. Then work the final 6 sts in checkerboard to correspond with left front shoulder. Bind off. Set aside.

5. Cast on 7 sts with blue yarn. Work stockinette stitch (K one row, P one row) for approximately 8" (or the lengthwise measurement of completed front section). Bind off.

6. Repeat step 5 for the other side of sweater front.

7. With RST, pin edges of navy stockinette strips to edges of front section. With navy yarn, hand-stitch seams closed at edges. Set aside.

Back:

1. Pick up front loops of the 24 single crochet stitches at top of back piece, tie on oatmeal yarn, and work checkerboard stitch for 16 rows.

2. On RS, work 6 sts checkerboard pattern and put remaining sts onto a stitch holder. Continue working the 6 sts for 7 more rows. Bind off.

3. Work checkerboard stitch across the 12 center sts, place them on a stitch holder, and continue to end of row.

4. Work 7 more rows of left back shoulder to correspond with completed right back shoulder. Bind off and set aside.

5. With blue yarn, cast on 7 sts and work stockinette stitch for approximately 8 inches (or lengthwise measurement of completed back section). Repeat for other back panel.

Neckline, shoulders, and bottom ribbing:

1. With number 3 needles, pick up 26 sts around front neckline (space 7 at each side of 12 center sts on holder). Tie on red yarn and work K1, P1 ribbing for 4 rows. Bind off loosely in ribbing.

2. At back neckline, pick up 24 sts (space 6 at each side of center 12 sts on holder). Tie on red yarn and work K1, P1 ribbing for 4 rows. Bind off loosely in ribbing.

3. Edge each front shoulder with 1 row SC. Edge each back shoulder with 2 rows SC. Work 3 evenly spaced buttonholes into second row.

4. Sew 3 buttons to front shoulder.

5. Button the buttons, and hand-stitch shoulders together at the sleeve edge where they lap.

6. With number 3 needles, on front bottom edge of sweater, pick up 36 sts (6 sts from each navy side panel and 24 from front loop of SC edging on sock). Work K1, P1 ribbing for 6 rows. Bind off loosely in ribbing. Repeat for back.

Assembly and finishing:

1. With the RST, sew side seams closed approximately 6" up from bottom edge (to accommodate sleeve that measures approximately 3½" from shoulder edge to underarm seam).

2. On WS, ease sleeves into their slots, matching patterns at shoulder and underarm. With navy yarn, hand-stitch together, catching front loop of SC sleeve edging. Steam press.

3. Work 24 individual popcorn stitches with oatmeal yarn and attach 6 to each navy side panel in front and back.

72

~SWEATER FROM ARGYLE SOCKS~

THERE ARE
STARS IN THE
SKY WHERE
ANGELS MEET,

TO TAKE WORN-OUT
SOCKS FROM
GROWN-UPS' FEET,

AND MAKE
SPECIAL
SWEATERS
FOR BABIES SO
SWEET.

Aran Overalls

A man's Aran sweater in an extra-large size was spotted at a thrift store and couldn't be passed by for two reasons. The natural wool yarn was absolutely beautiful, and free of any signs of wear. The workmanship and variety of stitches used by the knitter were superb. It took many hours of labor to produce such a masterpiece, and there it sat waiting to be rescued from the rag truck!

Because of the sweater's size, the sleeves were the only portion needed to fashion overalls in the 12-month size. These instructions, however, are general, and the basic concept applies to all sizes. Merely check the sleeves of your sweater against the jumpsuit pattern and/or your baby's measurements to be sure they will work. Measure the leg length as described in step 1 of the instructions, and cut off the sleeves to that length. The top raglan portion, then, becomes the bib.

Match the yarn used in the sweater as closely as possible with purchased yarn. If you are not pleased with the match, choose a contrasting color instead. The result in either case will not be a detraction, however. No one will pay any attention if the yarns do not match perfectly because the final product is so attractive. We made a long-sleeved, round-collared shirt of very soft cotton to go under the overalls, and lined the overalls with the same fabric.

You will need:

- 1 old adult-size sweater with long raglan sleeves
- 1 skein 4-ply knitting yarn, with the same fiber content as the old sweater
- 4 to 6 buttons, ½" diameter or larger
- size 5 knitting needles
- size G crochet hook
- ¾ yard soft cotton or cotton blend for optional lining
- darning or tapestry needle

74

Before you begin:

Read about the seed stitch, popcorn or bobble stitch, single crochet, and Scandinavian twisted ties in the Special Techniques section.

Determine which size knitting needles will give you a gauge close to that of the sweater. If you are going to follow our directions exactly, do a gauge swatch with 4-ply yarn and number 5 needles.

Instructions:

1. Use Basic Pattern II, pages 57-60.

2. On each sweater sleeve, measure the desired length of pant leg from ankle to crotch and add two inches. Cut the sleeves from the sweater at this point. Find a yarn end and unravel the knitting for about two inches, until you reach the correct leg length and have a good set of loops to pick up on the knitting needles.

3. Count the number of loops on each sleeve and divide them in half. Pick up half of the loops from one sleeve, then half of the loops from the second sleeve, onto one needle. Tie on your new yarn, and beginning on the right side, P 1 row, K 1 row, P 1 row. Bind off the next row in K.

4. Repeat for the second halves of the sleeves. Be sure to make the connecting stitch at the crotch very tight, as there will be a tendency for this section to loosen in tension. If necessary, reinforce the crotch by hand with a yarn-threaded needle so there are no gaps.

5. If you plan to line the overalls, cut lining for the legs at this point. Place the lining fabric on top of the completed overalls to get the shape, pin, and cut it ¼" extra around the edges for seam allowance. Sew side seams of legs; set aside.

6. Measure the distance you need for a bib from the crotch to the bib top. Measure this same distance down from each raglan sleeve top. Cut carefully at this point, trying to sever the knit **between** rows, if possible.

7. Overcast each raw edge with machine zigzag. Steam press to original shape.

8. If the raglan tops together are not wide enough to go around baby's girth, add width by picking up stitches on sides and knitting enough rows to give you the necessary width. Or use crochet, if you prefer.

9. Edge machine-finished raw edges of the bib with a row of single crochet. With RST and using a yarn-threaded needle, sew bibs to front and back of finished legs.

10. Cut linings for front and back bibs if you choose, and blindstitch to WS. Leave bottoms open. Attach leg linings with blindstitch, and blindstitch bib and leg linings together at leg tops.

11. For front pockets which blend nicely with an Aran pattern, work the following pattern: With the purchased yarn and #5 needles, CO 15 stitches.
 Rows 1 through 4: K1, P1 ribbing.
 Row 5: K1, P1, K1, P1, K1, P5, K1, P1, K1, P1, K1.
 *Row 6: P1, K1, P1, K1, P1, K5, P1, K1, P1, K1, P1.
 Row 7: Repeat Row 5.
 Row 8: Repeat Row 6.
 Row 9: K1, P1, K1, P1, K1, P2, work bobble in P, P2, K1, P1, K1, P1, K1.
 Rows 10 through 13: Work from * to Row 9.
 Rows 14 through 16: Work from * to Row 8.
 Bind off in the pattern. Repeat for the second pocket.

12. Hand-stitch pockets to bottom edge of bib with yarn.

13. The sides can be treated in two ways. They can be sewn together up to the waistline, or can be left open for more ease in putting the overalls on baby. If you choose to leave them open, make two Scandinavian twisted ties for each lower side.

14. Make two long Scandinavian twisted ties to thread through the front and back waistlines of the bib. These will gather the overalls to baby's waist and tie at the sides.

15. Make two Scandinavian twisted ties to thread through the ankle cuffs.

16. Knit the shoulder straps and crosspieces: CO 4 stitches and work seed stitch for length of shoulder strap. Bind off. Repeat for second strap. CO 4 stitches and work seed stitch for length of crosspieces (which connect shoulder straps at top of bib). Bind off.

17. Hand-stitch back shoulder straps to back bib with yarn. Hand-stitch back crosspiece to each shoulder strap and to top edge of back bib. Attach front straps and crosspieces in the same way.

18. Sew 3 buttons to each front strap. Work machine buttonholes to correspond with the bottom buttons.

75

HALF THE WORK THAT IS DONE IN THIS WORLD IS TO MAKE THINGS APPEAR WHAT THEY ARE NOT. ~ E. R. BEADLE

~ ARAN OVERALLS ~

~ WHEN IS A SWEATER NOT A SWEATER ?

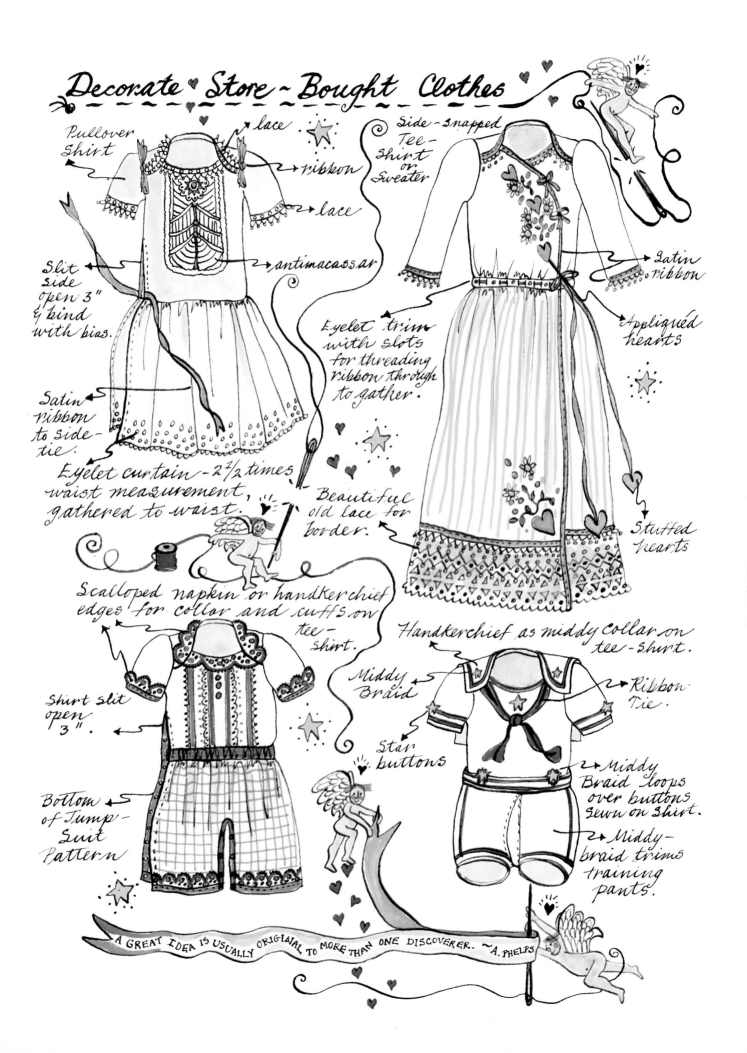

Decorate ♥ Store~Bought Clothes

Pullover Shirt

lace

ribbon

lace

antimacassar

Slit side open 3" & bind with bias.

Satin ribbon to side-tie.

Eyelet curtain - 2½ times waist measurement, gathered to waist.

Side-snapped Tee-Shirt or Sweater

Satin ribbon

Appliquéd hearts

Eyelet trim with slots for threading ribbon through to gather.

Beautiful old lace for border.

Stuffed hearts

Scalloped napkin or handkerchief edges for collar and cuffs on tee-shirt.

Shirt slit open 3".

Bottom of Jump-Suit Pattern

Handkerchief as middy collar on tee-shirt.

Middy Braid

Ribbon Tie.

Star buttons

Middy Braid loops over buttons sewn on shirt.

Middy-braid trims training pants.

A GREAT IDEA IS USUALLY ORIGINAL TO MORE THAN ONE DISCOVERER. ~A. PHELPS

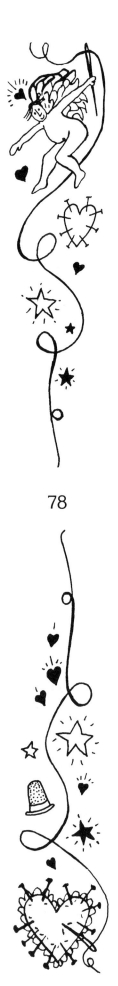

DECORATING PURCHASED CLOTHES

One of the easiest ways to expand your baby's wardrobe and make it truly unique is to decorate ready-made clothing, either new or used, by applying your own special touches. All the second-hand textile treasures which are incorporated into the projects in this book can be used with store-bought clothing, too. The five-and-dime has some wonderful bargains and, of course, thrift shops always have nearly new clothing at good prices.

Garments with simple lines are the most receptive to decoration. Plain overalls or the famous farmer-style suspendered pants are exciting canvases to which your needlework treasures can be stitched. Jumpers of the same simple style are manufactured for baby girls. See the illustration of decorated overalls on page 80 for some ideas.

Tiny sweatpants or knit drawstring pants can be turned into eye-catching animals. You can transform uninteresting pants into something special by adding face bibs. The face of the beast (cat, lamb, or bunny, for instance) becomes the front bib, and an unadorned copy of the face becomes the back of the animal's head, or the back bib. To these front and back heads are attached ears and the shoulder straps. A stuffed tail sewn onto the fanny completes the creature.

Tee shirts offer a fantastic variety of decorative opportunities. The addition of a collar changes the whole look of a shirt. Handkerchieves, laces, appliques, and trimmings can all be applied by hand or machine to give the shirt a different appearance. The illustrations on page 82 offer a few suggestions. When you have tried all your ideas for applied designs, try stenciling, painting, tie-dyeing or batik if you fancy painted techniques. The shirts are so tiny, they are marvelous for experimental artwork! A skirt, of either knit or woven fabric, can be attached to the bottom of a tee shirt to turn a boring tee into a charming dress, or jumpsuit legs can be added to make a little boy's bloomer-legged tee suit.

Sweaters and hooded sweatshirts are ideal backgrounds for applying heavier fabrics. Hoods make great "animal heads," as all sorts of ears (bunny, mouse, or cat) can be stitched to the hood. Matching tails at the center back and accents on the drawstrings, at the zipper-pull, and around the neck add to the whimsy. You might consider attaching color-coordinated mittens to the end of the sleeves as "paws."

A sweater can be transformed into a lovely dress or an elegant robe for a special occasion with the application of beautiful laces and ribbons, and the addition of a short or long skirt to the bottom. A casing at the waist allows for a drawstring tie closure. Look for vintage hand-knit baby sweaters for this design as they lend themselves superbly to this romantic approach. Do not pass them by just because they have tiny holes or stains. By top-stitching lace and ribbons to the sweater you can hide any imperfections and repair them at the same time.

Decorated Farmer-style Overalls

Oshkosh, Wisconsin, has become famous for the manufacture of high-quality work pants for the agricultural trades. For almost a century, Oshkosh overalls have been known to farmers as a rugged, long-wearing wardrobe staple. When the company began making miniature versions for babies, toddlers, and children, however, Oshkosh endeared itself to the nation's parents and became practically a household name.

Oshkosh overalls are wonderful just by themselves, but are also great for decorating. The overalls illustrated here are a copy of the famous originals. They were purchased new at a very reasonable price, and were chosen because the fabric is heavy, though not rigid—perfect for appliques, buttons, and hand-sewn sequins.

Two different old tea towels were used for the appliques. An Oriental hand-embroidered linen tea towel was chosen as the main source of applique because it had a little boy figure, flowers, and two animals embroidered on it, and because it had an embroidered scalloped edge. The other towel had appliqued and embroidered animals and flowers. Both were perfect in their unsophisticated charm.

The approach for this type of applied design is to cut out the desired embroidered areas and machine-applique them to the overalls in an arrangement which pleases you. The illustration shows one possible collage.

The scalloped edges were used to accent the front pockets. Because an infant has no need for the bib pocket which is a feature of this design, the front appliques are sewn right over it. The large silver button of that pocket becomes the sun when silver sequins are hand sewn in radiating lines from it. Sequins are also used to accent fir trees cut from green cotton and applied to the front and back. Heart appliques at the knees are optional, but are always a good idea for crawlers, as they add extra strength.

Novelty buttons in star, moon, bird, and frog shapes add final touches. Just be sure to sew them on very securely with strong buttonhole twist. The number and kind of applied accents you add will determine how carefully the garment will have to be washed.

You will need:

- 1 pair farmer-style overalls
- appliqued and/or embroidered tea towels, napkins, handkerchieves or any suitable textile
- scraps of cotton
- embroidery floss
- sequins (optional)
- novelty buttons (optional)

Instructions:

1. Pre-shrink overalls and all fabrics you plan to use for appliques.

2. Leaving about ¼" of the linen around edges of embroidery, cut out all appliques and arrange them onto front and back of overalls in a collage. Be aware of the side pockets and keep appliques clear of them, unless you plan to apply a design on just the top side. In this case, you will probably want to hand-stitch it.

3. Pin all designs in place. With machine set for zigzag applique, sew them to overalls on right side. Use as fine a stitch as possible.

4. Add your own embroidery where you wish—the more the better! Sew on sequins and novelty buttons very securely.

OVER ALL THE WATER, OVER ALL THE SEA, LET'S CATCH LITTLE FISHES FOR OUR MID-DAY TEA. A NURSERY RHYME.

~ FARMER OVERALLS ~

-BACK-

Decorate Store-Bought Clothes

Cardigan sweater (hand-knit—a Thrift shop find?) embellished with laces, ribbons, antimacassars, eyelet waist & long skirt.

Raglan-sleeved cardigan; Navy- or Royal-Blue, with rick-rack, mini pom-poms, appliqués, and star buttons.

Cardigan with new or old quilt sewn onto front and back hides imperfections. Heart buttons.

Hooded Sweatshirt becomes a bunny with ears on the hood. Add bunny tail at back & appliqués.

Sweatshirt becomes a cat with ears, tail, mouse & cheese appliqués, and mittens attached for "paws."

Sweat pants or knit pants or pajama bottoms become animals with faces as bibs.

~DECORATED~ TEE SHIRTS~

Embroidered Handkerchief, Lace Edgings, and Ruffles.

Bandana and Rick-Rack

Ribbon Binding and "Pearl" Buttons

Blanket-stitched edging & embroidery.

Appliquéd heart, "mouse" ribbon streamers, baby's name & embroidered French Knots.

BABY'S NAME

TEES FOR YOU...

THESE SHIRTS SUIT BABY TO A: "T"ee

...AND TEES FOR ME!

ACCESSORIES

For some unusual ways to accessorize baby's wardrobe, reach into the recesses of your imagination and expand upon the ideas illustrated in other sections of this book. Most accessories can make good use of scraps or small pieces of special textiles.

The angel piggy cradle quilt on pages 85-86 is a take-off on the angel piggy vest, with the additions of appliqued stars, a house, and some trees. It can be made larger than the dimensions given in the written instructions by merely adding length and width. The delicate angel and vine border design for a pillowcase or sheet edge can also be used to embellish any number of sewing projects.

Because it is such a clever design, the sunbonnet (pages 93-94) is included as an additional accessory even though a bonnet pattern appears with the christening dress. Based on an old hat found at a flea market, its ingenious flat shape is expandable and folds over to fit a baby's head as it grows. At the same time it offers wonderful possibilities for decoration on the brim (note the addition of a bill and google eyes in the illustration: instant duck!).

An old nursery rhyme reads: "Shoe the horse, and shoe the mare, but let the little colt go bare," and it is certainly difficult to argue that anything is more beautiful than a baby's chubby-toed feet. However, when you see how easy it is to design exquisite little shoes for a baby's first year, you will undoubtedly want to try your hand at a pair or two. The ballet slippers, boots, and espadrilles make lovely, unusual gifts for a newborn. Embellished with your needlework, the baby's initials and the date, you will create a cherished heirloom far more appealing than today's ubiquitous machine-made baby booties.

Bibs

Bibs are perfect for using tiny tidbits of fabric. The pattern on the next page is shown in two sizes: a small round bib for newborns and a larger one for older infants and toddlers. It is a basic style, therefore it offers the most possibilities for applied decorations. Any of the applique patterns throughout the book can be used here; or study the vest and tabard illustrations on page 46 for additional ideas. When you are thinking of appliques, consider using doilies or antimacassars as part of a design: as a sun or moon, as the center of a flower, as wheels for a vehicle. Small squeakers inserted between the layers of fabric add an auditory stimulus.

To make a simple bib, you need less than 1/3 yard of washable cotton or cotton blend fabric (even less if you choose to back the bib with terry toweling), a 12-inch square of polyfill batting, a package of single-fold bias tape, and scraps of fabrics and trims for decorations. The pattern includes 1/4" seam allowance, so you need only enlarge it onto paper. Cut out one front bib and one back bib of fabric and one bib of polyfill. After you have decorated the front of the bib as you wish, pin the front and back with the right sides together then the batting on the top. Stitch the three layers together with 1/4" seam allowance around the outside edges, leaving the neck open. Trim the seam allowance to 1/8", turn to the right side and press. Finish the neck with bias tape, leaving long ends to tie.

A nice variation of the basic pattern can be achieved using a special doily as a yoke to which a "skirt" is attached. Cut the bib pattern straight off at the lowest front neckline point for the skirt. Use the neckline as a guide for the hole you must cut in the doily. Gather the skirt to fit the round front bottom edge of the doily and hand-stitch it on from the back. An added attraction of this design is that you can easily make it into a sundress by lengthening it and attaching a couple of side ties!

Assorted Bibs

PRICELESS ARE MY RICHES WHEN MY BRAIN WITH FANCY TEEMS. ~ D. SNOWDEN

Stuffed cloth Carrots

This little Piggy is a STAR! ~ Appliqués and an embroidered message.

Appliqués, squeaker inside, quilted outlines.

A Special Lace Bib for a Special Day.

A lined embroidered Linen Dresser Scarf ~ Folded over.

Squeaker under face, Guardian Angel wings.

Embroidered Napkin folded over on the diagonal. ~

Yarn Fringe

Appliqued Ears, squeaker under nose & Google Eyes.

Small Bib for Newborns. Larger Bib for larger Babies. ~ 1 square = 1 inch

Appliquéd Hearts

CRADLE AND CRIB LINENS

You can use the applique patterns illustrated for the angel piggy vest (page 51) to make this soft and warm cradle quilt. Stars in the sky, a house banked by trees, and a burst of "heart-drops" in lieu of raindrops from the cloud add visual interest and extra areas for quilting detail.

This is a good place to use up scraps and to try your hand at quilting a rather short-term project. The small amount of quilting indicated in the instructions can be done very quickly. You may decide, however, to really fill in the blanks and turn out an heirloom quilt. Covering the whole quilt with tiny quilting stitches will take much longer, but will yield something truly cherishable.

After baby is out of the cradle, you can display the quilt on the nursery wall by sewing small plastic cafe rings at intervals along the top back for hanging. Or a casing can be hand-stitched along the top back to hold a rod for the same purpose.

The embroidered borders for a crib sheet or pillowcase are designed to be worked with embroidery floss and a few simple stitches. The design can be embroidered on a purchased sheet and case, or on a strip of fabric that will subsequently be sewn onto a handmade or purchased article. The delicate vine and angel motifs lend themselves to many other decorative uses. They would be beautiful on the border of a bassinet skirt. They can be used on clothing, of course, and you could also incorporate the design into a hand-painted edging for the woodwork in baby's room, or on the furniture.

Angel Piggy Cradle Quilt

Note:

Finished dimensions are approximately 34 inches long by 25 inches wide.

You will need:

- 1 yard 100% cotton fabric for quilt top
- 1 yard 100% cotton fabric for quilt back
- 1 yard polyester quilt batting
- assorted cotton scraps for appliques
- 1 package (3 yards) bias tape, ⅞" wide
- quilting thread
- quilting or large embroidery hoop, 10-12" diameter
- soft pencil (number 2 lead)

Instructions:

1. Cut quilt top to a rectangle 34" long by 25" wide. Find centers of length and width by folding quilt top in half; place a pin to mark each spot. Using a saucer or a salad plate as your guide, and paying attention to the center pin marks, lightly draw evenly spaced scallops along length and width of fabric with soft pencil. The corner scallops might be wider than those along the sides, depending upon size and number of scallops.

2. Cut the scallops along your pencil lines. Cut the quilt back and polyester batting the same.

3. Cut out appliques from scraps and pin them to quilt top as the illustration suggests, or in an arrangement of your own design.

4. With the machine set on zigzag applique stitch, sew the cut-outs to the quilt top. Or, turn under 1/16" around edges of the applique pieces, press, and blindstitch to quilt top with tiny hand stitches. Steam press.

5. Make a sandwich with the quilt back on the bottom (right side facing out), the quilt batting in the middle, and the quilt top on top. Pin layers together all around the scalloped edges.

6. Working from the center of the quilt to the outside edges, quilt the pattern you desire. Use the hoop for smooth, pucker-free quilting.

7. When the center appliques have been quilted, cut a paper pattern for the heart applique (use the angel piggy vest pattern on page 51, if you wish). With this as your guide, use a soft pencil to draw hearts into each scallop as in the illustration. Quilt around them as you reach the edges of the quilt.

8. Draw wavy lines for grassy hills under the house and for chimney smoke; quilt along these lines.

9. When your quilting is complete, pin raw edge of bias tape to edge of quilt with RST. Hand-stitch along manufacturer's fold line of bias tape (¼"). Fold bias tape to back side of quilt and pin. Blindstitch tape to back of quilt.

10. Embroider curly tails, eyes, and mouths onto the pigs. Embroider your name, baby's name, and the date somewhere on the quilt—for posterity.

11. Before using the quilt, wash gently to remove pencil marks.

Embroidered Borders for Crib Sheet and Pillowcase

Note:

A cradle or crib pillowcase measures approximately 16 by 12 inches. A standard crib mattress is 26 by 51 inches.

You will need:

- embroidery floss in greens, red, yellow, blue, pink, tan, orange
- purchased or handmade crib sheet and pillowcase
  or
  strip of soft cotton or linen 3½" high by the width you need
- small embroidery hoop, approximately 5" diameter
- embroidery needles
- tracing paper
- soft pencil (number 2 lead)

Instructions:

1. With a soft pencil, trace or copy onto tracing paper the embroidery design from the illustration on page 88. If you want a longer design, the vine can be picked up on either side of the sun and moon and continued ad infinitum.

2. With tape or weights, secure to a hard surface the fabric you are going to embroider. Turn tracing paper over so that the side with the pencil tracing is against fabric. Rub the design onto the fabric by scraping flat edge of pencil point over the lines, or by drawing over them again.

3. Stretch fabric over embroidery hoop and work the design with the stitches and colors of floss suggested in the illustration, or according to your own plan.

4. Attach the fabric strip to pillowcase or sheet. Before using the linens, wash them to remove pencil markings.

5. Consider embroidering the baby's initials somewhere in the design for a personalized heirloom look.

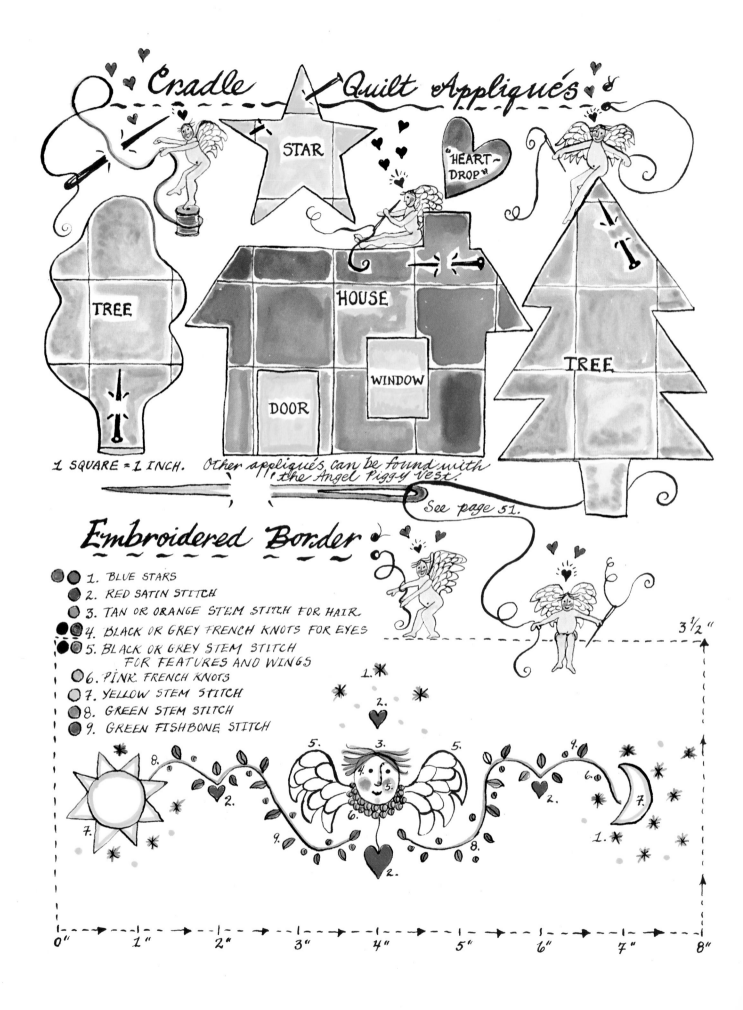

Cradle Quilt Appliqués

STAR

"HEART-DROP"

TREE

HOUSE

WINDOW

DOOR

TREE

1 SQUARE = 1 INCH.

Other appliqués can be found with the Angel Piggy Vest.

See page 51.

Embroidered Border

1. BLUE STARS
2. RED SATIN STITCH
3. TAN OR ORANGE STEM STITCH FOR HAIR
4. BLACK OR GREY FRENCH KNOTS FOR EYES
5. BLACK OR GREY STEM STITCH FOR FEATURES AND WINGS
6. PINK FRENCH KNOTS
7. YELLOW STEM STITCH
8. GREEN STEM STITCH
9. GREEN FISHBONE STITCH

3½"

0"   1"   2"   3"   4"   5"   6"   7"   8"

LITTLE BABY BLUE HAS LOST HER HOLIDAY SHOE. GIVE HER ANOTHER TO MATCH THE OTHER, AND THEN SHE WILL WALK IN TWO. AN OLD NURSERY RHYME.

~SHOES AND SLIPPERS~

SHOES AND SLIPPERS

Have needlework fun cobbling footwear for your baby's first year. Using a sole of soft leather (from old gloves or elbow patches?), crocheted string, or a double thickness of any heavy fabric, you can attach a variety of charming shoe tops.

The ballet slipper is not just for little girls! The use of dark, rich colors accented with flat grosgrain bows brings to mind traditional men's dress flats. They look elegant with a garment like the classic romper suit. A variation of the ballet slipper is the barefoot sandal. Felt works well for this design as it eliminates the need for overcasting cut edges, but any heavy fabric can be used. Cut out an arrangement of eyelets on the instep and finish their raw edges with buttonhole stitches.

Any fabric can be used for the espadrille. An easy approach is to embroider felt with colorful floss flowers and leaves. Consider using heavy cotton duck in primary colors. Using blanket stitch, sew it onto a crocheted string sole and tie it with a contrasting color of ribbon or twill tape. How eye-catching white eyelet over a brightly-hued cotton would be!

The third design is a boot. Old knits work well for all or part of a boot. The ankle cuff of older children's and adults' socks can be cut off and stitched to the sole to make wonderful slipper boots. The bottom of a sweater sleeve and cuffs can be incorporated onto a sole, too.

Most of us, at one time or another, have accidentally shrunk a wool sweater in the washing machine. Don't discard such a mistake! You have a textile that is called, among other things, "boiled wool," and it is ideal for little boots.

Before you begin making any footwear you should refer to the Special Techniques section, beginning on page 101, for information pertinent to your own project.

Ballet Slipper

You will need:

- 4" by 6" piece of soft leather, heavy felt, or double thickness of fabric for a sole
- approximately 1/3 yard medium to heavy felt
- 12" single-fold bias tape for binding the top shoe edge (optional)
- 18" ribbon, 1/4" wide for ankle ties (optional)
- assorted embroidery floss and trimmings

Instructions:

A note before beginning: The shoe pattern pieces all have ¼" seam allowances included in the dimensions. When seams are butted together, as with felt, the seam allowance should be trimmed off. Pattern pieces may also be prepared for butted seams in the following manner: Cut two of each pattern piece, sew them with right sides together and with ¼" seam allowances. Leave a 1" opening for turning. Trim the seam allowances to ⅛", turn to the right side and close the opening with blind stitches. Press.

1. Enlarge the pattern pieces and trim ¼" SA from each. Cut four of the slipper pattern piece and two soles, or double them if you wish a sturdier shoe.

2. Embellish each piece of felt with embroidery stitches, sequins, buttons, or trimmings.

3. With embroidery floss, use a fine blanket stitch to edge each piece of felt.

4. With embroidery floss, sew the center front toe seam closed by catching the "floating" thread of the blanket stitch edging on each side.

5. Hold bottom of this seam against CF of sole and sew top of shoe to sole, working from CF to CB on one side, then from CF to CB on the other side. Sew CB seam.

6. An alternate finish for the top edge of the shoe is to bind it with bias tape.

7. For an ankle tie, cut a length of colorful ribbon or cord and secure it firmly at the CB. Or make two buttonholes one inch apart at the center back for threading the ribbon through.

Espadrille:

You will need:

- 1 ball white cotton string: "parcel post twine" or heavy crochet thread
- size 1 crochet hook
- approximately 1/3 yard of hand-washable fabric for heels and toes
- 1/3 yard iron-on interfacing (optional)
- embroidery floss
- grosgrain or satin ribbon for ankle ties

Instructions:

1. Enlarge the paper pattern. Trim off the ¼" SA from the sole.

2. Using the paper sole pattern as a guide, crochet the sole with cotton string. Begin at either heel or toe end, and work single crochet in horizontal rows from one side of sole to the other. Do not be concerned if the shape is not perfect. Err on the small side.

3. When you have a sole which pleases you, do an edging of single crochet all around its perimeter. Repeat for the second sole.

4. Cut two toes and two heels from hand-washable fabric. Interface one side of each if necessary. Embroider the right side if you wish.

5. With RST, sew the two heel and two toe pieces with ¼" SA, leaving an opening along the flat edges of each to turn to the RS.

6. Turn, press, and blind-stitch the opening shut. As an alternative, you could bind the raw edges with bias tape.

7. Match the CF of the toe and heel with the center toe and heel points on the sole, and hand-stitch them together with embroidery floss.

8. For ankle ties, stitch ribbon to the back top of the heels, or work two buttonholes one inch apart through which ribbon can be threaded.

Boot:

You will need:

- approximately 1/3 yard shrunken wool or felt
- approximately 1/3 yard soft fabric for lining (optional)
- assorted embroidery floss and/or crewel yarns
- yarns for Scandinavian twisted ties or braided ties
- tassels or mini pom-poms for ends of ties

Instructions for unlined boots:

1. Enlarge the patterns and trim off ¼" SA from each piece. Cut from fabric one sole, two toes, and one heel for each boot.

2. Edge all pattern pieces with blanket stitch.

3. Embroider designs on the pieces as you desire.

4. Sew the CF toe seams closed by catching the "floating" thread of the blanket stitch edging on each side.

5. Match the CF of toe piece with the CF of the sole and stitch together.

6. Match the CB of the heel with CB heel point on the sole and stitch together.

7. Sew each bottom side of the toe to each side heel piece.

8. The CF opening at the ankles can be closed with Scandinavian twisted ties laced through the blanket stitch edging, or tiny grommets can be hammered on for lace carriers, or the edges can be folded back to reveal the optional lining.

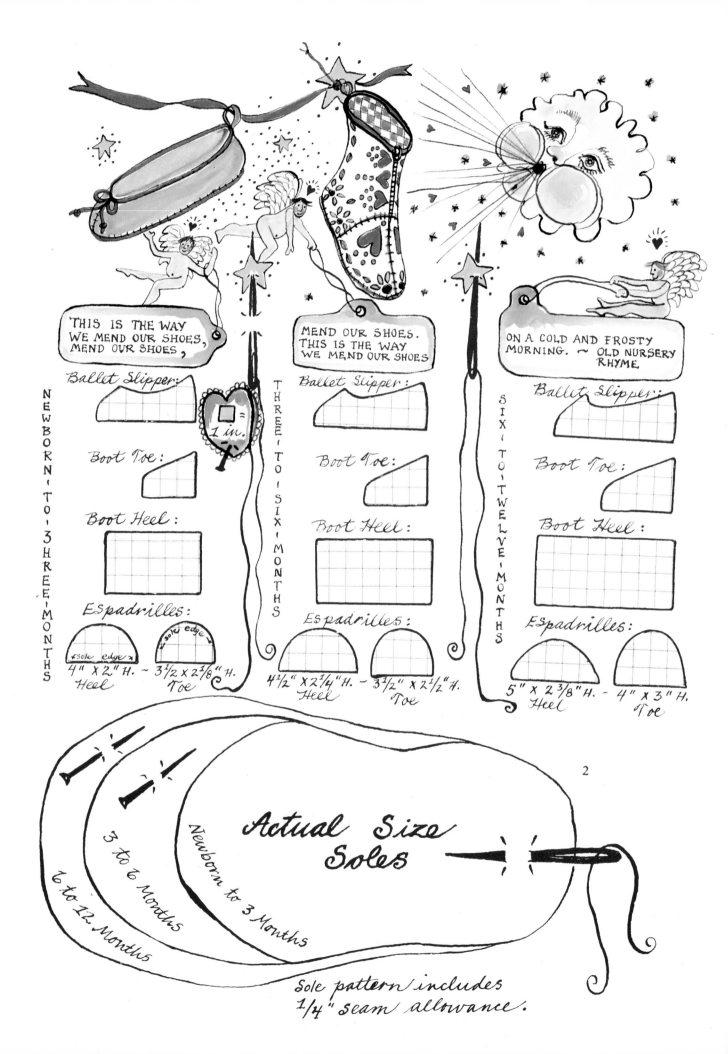

THIS IS THE WAY WE MEND OUR SHOES, MEND OUR SHOES,

MEND OUR SHOES. THIS IS THE WAY WE MEND OUR SHOES

ON A COLD AND FROSTY MORNING. ~ OLD NURSERY RHYME.

NEWBORN·TO·3HREE·MONTHS

THREE·TO·SIX·MONTHS

SIX·TO·TWELVE·MONTHS

Ballet Slipper:

Boot Toe:

Boot Heel:

Espadrilles:

1 in.

←sole edge→   ←sole edge→

4" X 2" H. ~ 3½ x 2⅛" H.
Heel   Toe

4½" X 2¼" H. ~ 3½" X 2½" H.
Heel   Toe

5" X 2⅜" H. ~ 4" X 3" H.
Heel   Toe

Actual Size Soles

Newborn to 3 Months

3 to 6 Months

6 to 12 Months

2

Sole pattern includes ¼" seam allowance.

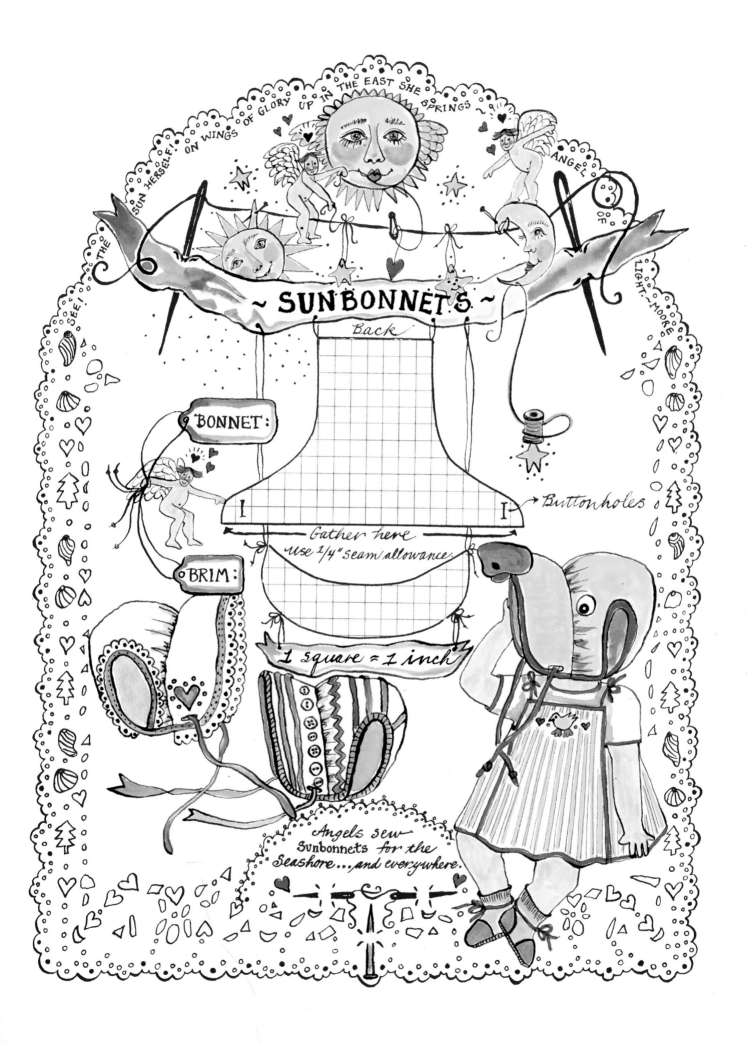

~ SUNBONNETS ~

SEE! THE SUN HERSELF! ON WINGS OF GLORY UP IN THE EAST SHE SPRINGS

ANGEL OF LIGHT — MOORE

Back

BONNET:

BRIM:

I   I

Gather here

Use ¼" seam allowance.

→ Buttonholes

1 square = 1 inch

Angels sew
Sunbonnets for the
Seashore...and everywhere.

Sunbonnet

The pattern for this versatile hat is adapted from an old one discovered at a flea market. Because two ties from the back of the bonnet thread through two buttonholes at either side of the brim, the hat fits a child of almost any age, from a baby up to a three-year-old toddler. If the bonnet seems too large for your new infant, shortening the back bottom edge and/or taking a tuck at the center back will compensate nicely.

The illustrations show several variations you can achieve from the same pattern and with some inspiration you will undoubtedly come up with many more ideas!

After you have tried the design for the season it was intended (summer), you might want to experiment with wool, corduroy, or other fabrics for cold weather. Or with lining the hat to see the difference in fit extra fabric makes. The only alteration you will have to make for a cold weather hat is the addition of a piece to cover each side of the head where the airy split occurs. The best way to determine the size of this piece is to try the sunbonnet on baby and then experiment until you find the gusset size that will fit your baby's head. You will probably want to line the bonnet for cold weather, so seam allowances of ¼" can be used throughout.

You will need:

- ½ yard washable 100% cotton or cotton blend fabric
- 2 packages single-fold bias tape
- 6" by 8" piece of iron-on interfacing for brim
- scrap fabrics
- buttons, or sew-on animal eyes

Instructions:

1. Enlarge the pattern on page 93, and cut from the fabric one pattern piece for bonnet and two pieces for brim. Cut one piece of iron-on interfacing for brim.

2. Bind the two curved sides of bonnet with bias tape. Bind the back flat edge of bonnet with bias tape, leaving 18" ends on both sides for ties.

3. Run a line of gathering stitches along front raw edge.

4. Apply iron-on interfacing to WS of one piece of brim fabric, then with RST, sew around the outside edge using ¼" SA. Trim to ⅛", turn to the right side and press.

5. Gather raw edge of bonnet to fit raw edge curve of brim and pin, with RST.

6. Machine-stitch the brim and bonnet back along this line, using ¼" SA. Press SA toward brim. Lay bias tape over seam, pin, and top-stitch it down along each folded edge. Be sure to fold raw edges of the bias tape under at each end.

7. Stitch a buttonhole at each side of bonnet brim to thread ties through.

8. Add appliques and trimmings to the brim and bonnet as you desire.

Soft Toys

One very simple pattern allows you to design a multitude of soft toys for baby. The senses of sight, sound, and touch can all be nurtured, depending upon the design of your toy.

Sewn up in bright colors, the toys are visually stimulating. Washable squeakers, found in most good craft supply stores, can be inserted within the polyfill stuffing to emit a sweet "squeak" when baby squeezes or bites the toys. The small arms, legs, and "handles" are just the right size for tiny fingers to grasp. Although the basic shape is designed to a scale suitable for infants, it can be enlarged to offer toy-making possibilities for many years of older childhood.

You will need:

- scraps of soft washable fabrics
- scraps of diminutive trimmings (narrow laces, narrow ribbons, tassels, mini pom-poms)
- satin ribbon, 1/16" wide, for necklines
- polyester filling
- small washable squeakers
- embroidery floss for features
- yarn or crochet thread for hair
- strong thread such as buttonhole twist for attaching accents

Instructions:

1. Enlarge pattern (page 96) and cut pattern pieces out of your fabric. Depending upon your design, you will need all or some of the following: two bodies, four arms, four legs, four ears, two tails, two trunks, two bodices (if your toy will have clothing). For dolls with clothes, the dotted neckline indicates where a bodice can be zigzag appliqued to the basic body pattern. Cut the arms from the same fabric as the bodice for a long-sleeved "garment" or from the body fabric for a sleeveless look. The same holds true for legs.

2. To clothe the doll, applique bodice to body at dotted neckline. Straight-stitch it along sides and bottom edge ⅛" from the raw edges. Mark arm set-in points.

3. With RST and using ¼" SA, sew body together. Leave openings at arm markings and across bottom. Turn to the outside and press, folding SA into armholes as you do.

4. Assemble arms and legs with RST and ¼" SA. Leave the short, flat edges open so you can turn them to right side and stuff with polyfill. Sew closed at flat edges.

5. Pin ends of stuffed arms into bodice armholes and blind-stitch closed.

6. With RST, pin stuffed legs along their flat edges to only the **front** lower opening of the bodice. Machine or hand-stitch.

7. Stuff the body loosely with polyfill. Turn back the lower back edge of the body ¼", pin to the top backs of legs, and blind-stitch closed.

8. Embroider the features. Use French knots for eyes and bellybuttons. Whiskers are French knots with thread tails left on.

9. If your toy is an animal, sew ears, trunks, tails, or other three-dimensional features as you did the arms and legs. Because the pieces are so small, the seam allowance should be adequate stuffing. Turn the raw edges under and hand-stitch them securely to the toy wherever your design dictates.

10. Fashion hair with yarn or crochet cotton.

11. Blind-stitch tiny ribbon, gathered lace, or ribbon streamers around necklines if definition is needed.

12. Apply trimmings where you desire, but keep everything simple.

13. Be sure all trimmings and accents on baby toys are sewn **very securely**.

Toys: all made from one basic shape:

Tan or white or grey tee shirt knit

Pink satin

Grey Knit

Pink Satin

Solid

French Knots with tails for whiskers.

French Knot Belly Button

Mouse ribbon

Cord tail Knotted at end.

Pattern: 1 square = 1 inch.

Short arm

Short leg

Use 1/4" seam allowance.

Mini pom-pom or French Knots.

Any soft fabric ~ gingham?

Mini Pom-pom

French Knots

Yarn or Crochet thread

Ribbons

Gathered lace.

Calico

Dark Socks for skin.

Basic shape turned on its side can be any four-legged creature!

Scrap fabrics.

Make several & snap the hands together for older children.

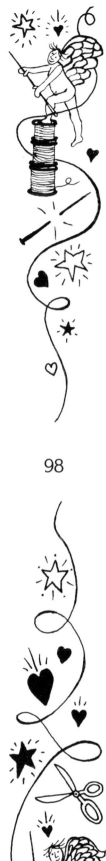

Squeaky Teething Toys

This versatile accessory uses a basic shape, such as the heart, star, or circle, as a "container" for a washable squeaker. Stuffing is pushed into the shape and nestled around the squeaker. When you sew the stuffed shape onto a stuffed fabric handle, you have a rattle-shaped teether which emits a small squeak when baby squeezes or bites on it.

Large, colorful, baby-safe plastic bells, available in some craft stores, can make the teething toy a true rattle. Be sure to secure the bell tightly to the outside of the fabric handle. Ribbons tied onto the teether at the end look very special and add movement as the baby shakes it.

The squeaky toy makes a perfect baby gift—it is only a slight exaggeration to say you can have one practically finished in the time it takes to read through the instructions!

You will need:

- scraps of colorful, washable fabrics; 100% cotton or cotton blends are best
- narrow satin ribbons
- small washable squeakers
- scrap trimmings
- embroidery floss
- strong thread, such as buttonhole twist, for attaching ribbons and optional plastic bells
- large plastic bells (optional)

Instructions:

1. The teether shapes illustrated are approximately three inches square. On a piece of paper draw a 4" graph of 1" squares. Fold the paper in half, matching up the grids, and draw half the shape you wish to use. For a star, round off the points to make it "fat," as this will make a more attractive finished product than will a pointy star. Cut out the shape on the fold. When you open the paper your shape will be symmetrical. Cut two pattern pieces from your fabric scraps.

2. Leave ½" open at the center bottom of the heart, star, or circle as you sew the RST with ¼" SA. Trim SA to ⅛", and turn to the right side. Press.

3. Insert a washable squeaker and stuff the shape with polyfill. Do not stuff too tightly, as the area around the squeaker hole has to be somewhat free to emit a noise. Squeeze the shape as you stuff it to make sure the squeaker is still working when the teether is ready to sew onto the handle.

4. Cut a strip of fabric 4½" long by 1" wide for the handle. Fold RST, and sew a tube with ⅛" SA from top to bottom, closing one end. Turn to RS and stuff as firmly as possible with polyfill.

5. Insert top of handle about ½" into hole at bottom of squeaker-filled shape. Pin, then hand-sew the two firmly together with strong thread.

6. Sew on colorful ribbons and a bell, if you desire. If you have made a circle shape which will be a face (see illustration), embroider the features, tie on yarn hair, and make a little cone hat. Gathered lace at the neckline and ribbon streamers add pretty finishing touches.

Guardian Angel (illustrated opposite page 1)

Hanging by a satin ribbon on baby's nursery door, this guardian angel announces that some-one very special slumbers within. There are many other charming ways you might display this stuffed decoration: hanging from baby's window lock and dangling in the sunlight, as a shade pull, or as a wall accent over baby's bed. Three to five angels can be grouped as a mobile above the cradle or crib. Hanging on the wall over the baby's changing table, or from it, the angel could be used as a pin cushion.

You will undoubtedly come up with other imaginative ways to use this versatile pattern. Consider it as a stencil for baby's walls or furniture, as an applique design for one of the garment patterns in this book, or perhaps nestled in a delicate grapevine wreath.

You will need:

- ¼ yard unbleached cotton muslin, or black or brown cotton
- scrap of quilt batting, to fit the wing pattern piece
- polyfill
- embroidery floss, for facial features
- for hair: fleece (real or artificial), or very fuzzy wool yarn
- approximately 15" white or off-white lace, ¼" wide, to define the angel's neck.

Instructions:

1. Enlarge and cut pattern (page 100) from muslin: two bodies, two wings, four arms. Cut one wing piece from quilt batting. The pattern dimensions include ⅛" seam allowance.

2. On the piece which will be back side of angel, with a hard, sharp pencil lightly draw the line separating the legs.

3. Set machine at a very fine stitch, pin RST, and sew the two bodies together, leaving top (back) open where short lines indicate. The wing will be inserted into this opening.

4. Clip corners, turn to right side, and top-stitch line which separates legs, making sure the beginning and end of your stitching is secured firmly. Set aside.

5. Layer the two wing pattern pieces and the one wing piece of quilt batting on top. Pin the three layers together and sew them with ⅛" seam allowance, leaving the bottom (straight edge) open. Turn and press.

6. Top-stitch line which divides the wing in two (dotted line).

7. On the side of the wing which will be in back, use a hard, sharp pencil to lightly draw "feathers." Top-stitch along the lines, securing thread ends firmly.

8. Fold smaller wing section back along stitching line. Stitch in place at bottom.

9. With RST, place flat raw edge of wing against the **front** raw open edge of the body. Stitch across. Do not secure the back body of the angel with the stitches.

10. Stuff the feet, legs, and body with polyfill. Turn under raw edge of back opening ⅛", pin, and blind-stitch it closed across back of wing, hiding original machine stitches as you sew.

11. With RST, machine-stitch around arms leaving about 1¼" open at the rounded tops. Turn to RS and stuff with polyfill.

12. Turn under rounded raw edges ⅛" and blind-stitch closed. Pin arms to angel in whatever position you wish—both arms upraised, one down and one up, etc. Blind-stitch arms to body.

13. Gather lace to fit around neckline and blind-stitch with tiny stitches.

14. Embroider facial features and a bellybutton.

15. Attach hair as you desire. A fuzzy white yarn, frayed and frizzled, is especially fun for a rather humorous, risque-looking angel. Tight little French knots in black yarn would be perfect for a black angel done up in black or brown muslin.

99

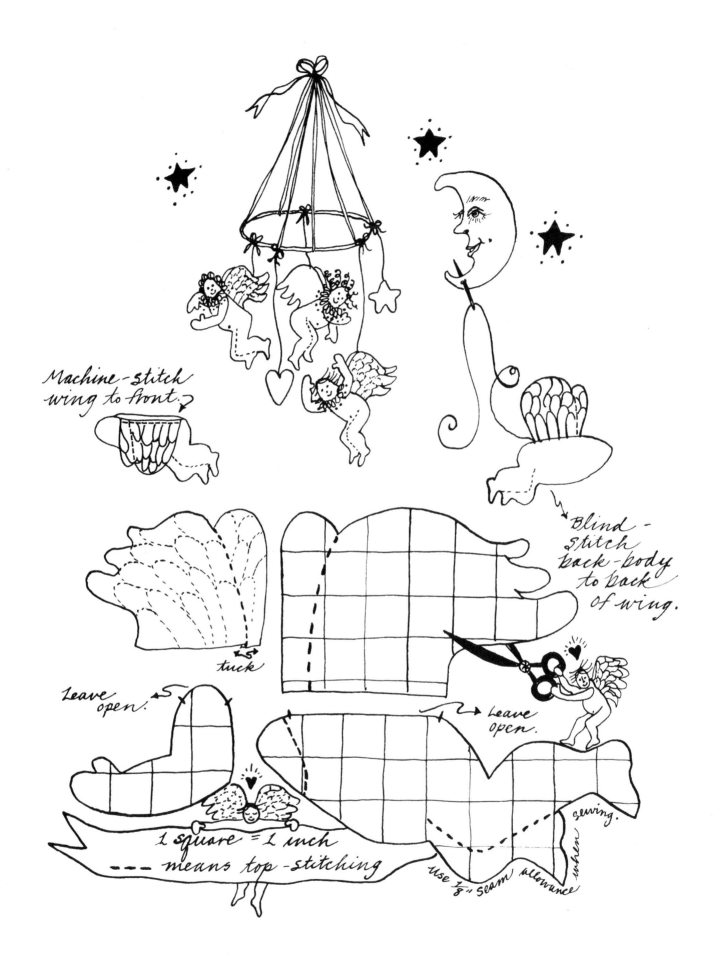

Machine-stitch
wing to front.

Blind-
stitch
back-body
to back
of wing.

tuck

Leave
open.

Leave
open.

1 square = 1 inch
----- means top-stitching

use ⅞" seam allowance   when sewing.

SPECIAL TECHNIQUES

SEWING TECHNIQUES

If you've read this far you probably are an experienced sewer, and familiar with the sewing techniques described in this section. For review or slightly different approaches, however, you might benefit from reading the explanations on the following pages.

BIAS TAPE FINISHES FOR SLEEVES, NECKLINES, AND HEMS

Single-fold bias tape is easy to work with and makes a versatile finish for many of the garments in this book. Using a manufactured bias means that the finish will be a contrast to the fabric you are using. If you wish the finish to match your garment, you can cut bias strips to the width you prefer, but plan on extra yardage to do this. Cutting bias strips uses a lot of fabric!

If you want drawstrings in the sleeves and the hems, decide where you would like the ties to appear, top seam, sleeve sides, or bottom seam of the sleeve? Center front, center back, or side seam of the hems?

Open the bias tape flat, fold one end ½" to inside, and pin right side of the folded edge to wrong side of the sleeve or hem seamline. This will be the entry for the drawstring. Pin the bias tape on the manufacturer's fold line (¼") around the edge to be finished. When you reach the beginning point, fold the raw end over ½", cut off, and pin right next to the first folded edge. Machine-stitch. Turn the bias tape to right side of the garment, folding on the stitch line, and pin up the width of the tape. The two ½" folds you made at the beginning and end form a "buttonhole" for drawstrings to enter and exit. You may also want to top-stitch the bottom edges of the bias tape for a very professional look. See illustrations as a guide.

If you wish to use drawstring hem finishes on jumpsuit legs, a little more care will have to be taken. After the crotch has been finished (see next section), cut, or make from yarn, two drawstrings for each leg. Each one should measure approximately 9 to 10" (the width of the front or back of the leg plus a little extra). Pin to the right side of the garment at each end of each pant leg, ¼" in from the folded edge of the crotch finish. Sew down securely. See illustration.

Open the bias tape flat, fold over the end raw edge ½" and pin this folded edge against the finished edge of the bottom leg (end of crotch finish) with the right side of the bias tape against the wrong side of the garment. Pin ¼" (bias tape manufacturer's fold line) from the edge to the side seam. Fold over ½" and cut off bias tape. Pin edge to the seam line. Repeat for the other half of the leg, making sure the two folded edges at the side seam touch. Machine-stitch along the fold line, avoiding the drawstrings you have previously stitched to the bottom crotch leg edges. Turn up the right side of the bias along fold (stitch) line and press. Pin the bias tape to the right side of the legs, making sure that the drawstrings are inside the casing and each end is outside the buttonhole which formed at the side seams with the two folded tape ends. Be **sure** the drawstring is in the middle of the casing, so when you machine-stitch the bias casing to the leg, you won't catch the drawstring. Carefully machine-stitch the casing in place.

BIAS TAPE FINISHES FOR CENTER FRONT, CENTER BACK, AND PANTS CROTCH

Single-fold bias tape works well for these finishes also, and is wide enough to use with snaps or hooks and eyes as fasteners. If you are going to use buttons and buttonholes, you will need wider bias tape or will have to cut bias strips of your fabric. You can use straight-of-grain strips, rather than bias, for straight-of-grain edges, like the center front and center back, to give extra firmness. You must, of course, use bias for any curved edges.

If the garment opens all the way to the hemline, start at the bottom and pin right side of the lengthwise edge of bias tape or strip to the wrong side of the garment edge. Stitch ¼" from the edge (on the manufacturer's fold line). Fold to right side along stitching line and press. Pin, then machine-stitch. If you want the bias tape to appear on the wrong side of the garment rather than on the right, just reverse the directions and place bias tape and fabric with the right sides together.

If the garment opens only part way down the center front or center back, both pattern pieces can be cut out on a fold. The opening can then be cut and bound with bias tape. If the open-

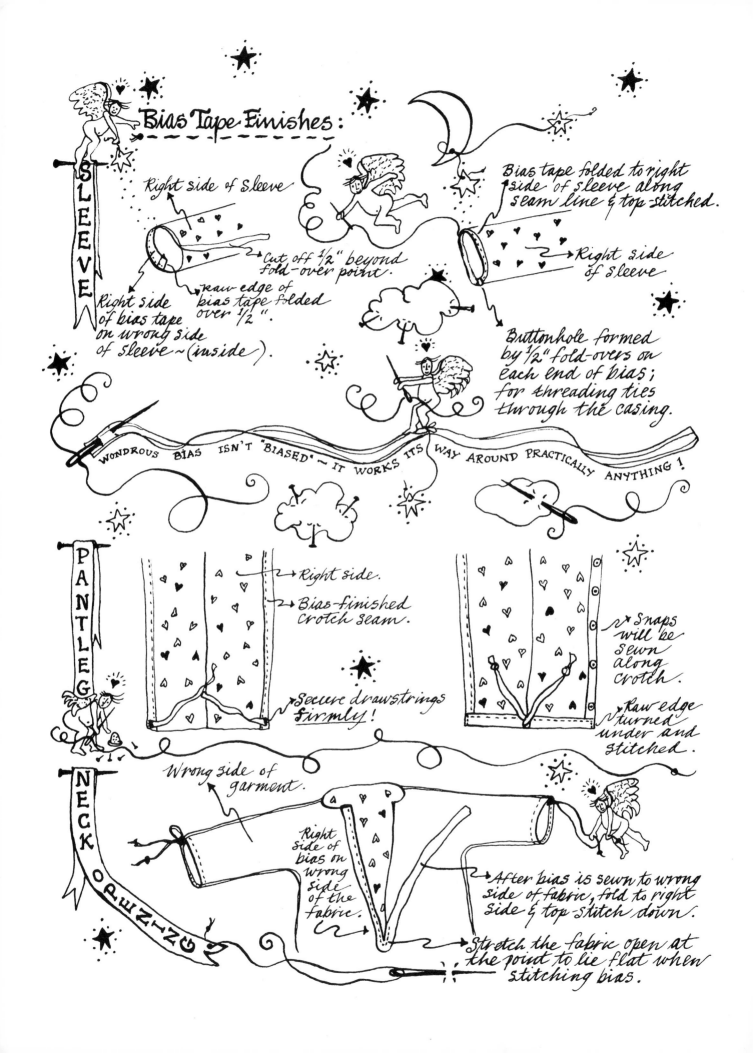

Bias Tape Finishes:

SLEEVE

Right side of Sleeve

Cut off ½" beyond fold-over point.

Raw edge of bias tape folded over ½".

Right side of bias tape on wrong side of sleeve ~ (inside).

Bias tape folded to right side of sleeve along seam line & top-stitched.

Right side of sleeve

Buttonhole formed by ½" fold-overs on each end of bias; for threading ties through the casing.

WONDROUS BIAS ISN'T "BIASED" ~ IT WORKS ITS WAY AROUND PRACTICALLY ANYTHING!

PANTLEG

Right side.

Bias-finished crotch seam.

Secure drawstrings firmly!

Snaps will be sewn along crotch.

Raw edge turned under and stitched.

NECK LINE

Wrong side of garment.

Right side of bias on wrong side of the fabric.

After bias is sewn to wrong side of fabric, fold to right side & top stitch down.

Stretch the fabric open at the point to lie flat when stitching bias.

ing will be in a seamline, the seam can be sewn close to the point you wish the opening to begin, and then bound off. See illustrations.

If you want ties as closures, mark their placement points with pins on the right side of the garment after the bias tape has been pinned but before it is stitched down. Tuck the ties into the folded-over bias tape edge and pin down. Then as you sew the bias edge to the right side of the garment, you will also be catching the ties with your machine-stitching.

The pants crotch finish is approached in exactly the same manner except that you **must** use bias tape or strips, not straight-of-grain fabric. If the pants are long you will want to use at least seven snaps for a draft-free closure: one at the center seam and six spaced evenly along the opening. Short pants will, of course, require fewer. You may want to try the ready-made snap tape which is available in most sewing stores. Its only drawback is the limited choice of colors.

NECKLINE FINISHES

You can have a wonderful time designing neckline finishes! Something as simple as a contrasting bias tape finish (applied in the same manner as for sleeve and hem finishes, described in the preceding section) might be all you want. But then there are collars to consider!

There are many styles of collars which can be attached to the neckline of the basic gown or jumpsuit after the garment's opening has been finished. Following are instructions for making several different collars.

Round or petal collar

Construct the collar: sew right sides together, trim seam to ⅛", turn and press. If you are using woven fabric, you may wish to bind outer edges with bias tape instead of seaming them. If your collar will be trimmed with lace, you may want to use just a single thickness of collar fabric.

Pin right side of collar to the right side of garment at the center front and center back and then in between. Pin, then baste ⅛" from raw edge. Cut a strip of bias tape the length of the neckline plus 1". Pin the wrong side of the bias tape on top of the collar edge you have just stitched, turning in the tape ends ½" at edges of neck opening. Machine-stitch down ¼" in from the raw edge. Trim to ⅛".

103

Turn the bias to wrong side of neck opening and top-stitch along collar edge. Pulling to stretch the bias along the curve, pin it to neckline. Machine-stitch, making sure to sew the folded neck opening edges closed. See illustrations.

Flaps collar

Following the neckline curve of the collar pattern on page 32, you can draft any number of unusual collars to finish off your garment. Cut two pieces for each flap and treat each one as a collar, or bind single thicknesses with colorful bias tape. Space them around the neckline and finish off as previously instructed for the round or petal collar. See illustration.

Mandarin collar

This collar variation is very easy to execute. Besides working well with the basic patterns in this book, it offers two particularly good features: extra warmth around baby's neck and a wonderful place for attaching hoods and hats. Hoods and hats can be tied on, snapped on, fastened on with hooks and eyes, or buttoned on.

Measure the length of the garment neckline you wish to give the mandarin collar. Draw out this length on a piece of paper and add ¼" at each end. Mark the center front or center back (the opposite of where the opening will be), and at this point indicate the height you wish the collar to be. A delicate mandarin is approximately ¾"; 1" to 1¼" is a good height for attaching headgear. All measurements depend upon your baby's neck size—and number of chins. Extend this point parallel to the neckline until 1½" from the end, then make a curve down to the neckline. See illustrations.

If your fabric is lightweight, cut two collar pieces of the fabric and one of interfacing (the iron-on kind is a good choice). Press or baste interfacing to wrong side of collar, then with right sides together, using ¼" seam allowance, sew outside edges to ¼" from neck edge. Turn and press.

Pin one collar raw edge to the right side of the center back (or comparable point, depending on your neck opening), then around the neckline. You will be straightening the garment's

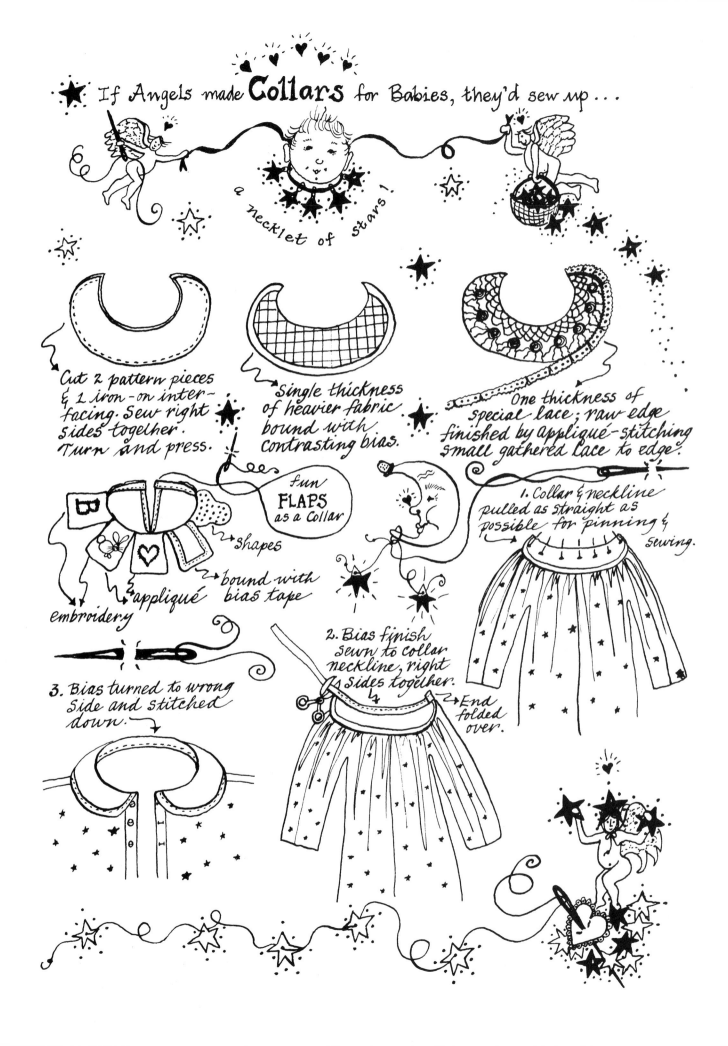

If Angels made **Collars** for Babies, they'd sew up...

a necklet of stars!

Cut 2 pattern pieces & 1 iron-on interfacing. Sew right sides together. Turn and press.

Single thickness of heavier fabric bound with contrasting bias.

One thickness of special lace; raw edge finished by appliqué-stitching small gathered lace to edge.

fun FLAPS as a Collar

→ Shapes

→ bound with bias tape

appliqué

embroidery

B

1. Collar & neckline pulled as straight as possible for pinning & sewing.

2. Bias finish sewn to collar neckline, right sides together.
→ End folded over.

3. Bias turned to wrong side and stitched down.

curved neckline to fit the straight edge of the collar as you pin. Machine-stitch ¼" seam. Pin the other raw edge of the mandarin collar to the neckline at or just below the previous line of stitching. Finish by hand with blind stitch, and press. See illustrations.

Ruffled collar

A lovely soft and feminine look is achieved with this simple collar. Merely multiply the neckline measurement times two or two and a half, depending upon how full you wish the ruffle to be. Decide upon the width (height) you want (1" is good), and cut a length of fabric on the fold to get a double of the collar. For a stiffer ruffle, bind a single thickness with bias tape.

Fold right sides together and sew the ends closed with ¼" seam allowance. Turn and press. Run a line of machine basting ⅛ to ¼" up from raw edges, sewing them together. Gather to length of neckline. Pin ruffle in place along neckline with right sides together and machine-baste along the same line of stitching. Finish with bias tape or bias fabric strips as described for the round or petal collar. See illustrations.

SEAMS

French seams

These are excellent for baby clothes because they leave no raw edges on the inside of the garment—a good feature when a garment must be washed often.

To make a French seam, pin **wrong** sides together and sew ¼" from the raw edge from bottom to top. Trim seam allowance to ⅛". Turn the garment inside out (right sides together) and press along the seam. Stitch, from bottom to top, ¼" from the pressed seam edge, enclosing the first seam. You have sewn the required ½" seam allowance, and no raw edge is exposed. See illustration.

Overcast seams

Sometimes a French seam isn't the best approach. With heavy wool, for example, French seams would be too bulky. In this case it would be better to sew the seam in the regular manner and to machine-overcast each seam allowance before the seam has been pressed open. Or, if the fabric is not too thick, trim the seam allowance to ¼" and overcast both seams together. See illustrations.

Bias tape top-stitched seams

This seam treatment is a colorful way to accent outfits for baby. Sew the seams with **wrong** sides together, using ½" seam allowance. Trim the seam allowance to ¼" and press open. Pin single-fold bias tape over the seam, and from bottom to top, top-stitch as close as possible to each folded edge of the bias. Press. The wrong side of the garment will have no seam allowance showing. See illustrations.

HANDSEWN HEMS

There are two simple ways to prepare a raw edge for a handsewn hem. One way is to turn the edge ¼" toward the wrong side, press, and turn the folded edge up again to the depth of the finished hem. Pin in place. The second is to turn up the raw edge ¼", machine-stitch it, then press and pin to the finished length.

The three hemming stitches we find useful for a sturdy hold against baby's kicking feet are the blindstitch, the knotted blindstitch, and the hemming blanket stitch. Specific techniques are shown in the illustrations on page 108.

EMBELLISHMENTS

MOCK TATTING

Mock tatting is a variation of the thread loop belt carriers found on dresses, and is worked just like crocheted chain stitch, but with needle and thread. With this technique you can quickly and easily make a lacelike edging that resembles traditional tatting and provides a charming decorative addition to collars, cuffs, and neck openings. With your needle and thread, just catch the edge of the collar, say, along the seamline. Put the needle between the layers of the fabric about ½" from the starting point, bring it up at the starting point, pulling the end of the thread until it disappears into the inside of the collar. Catch a small piece of the collar edge

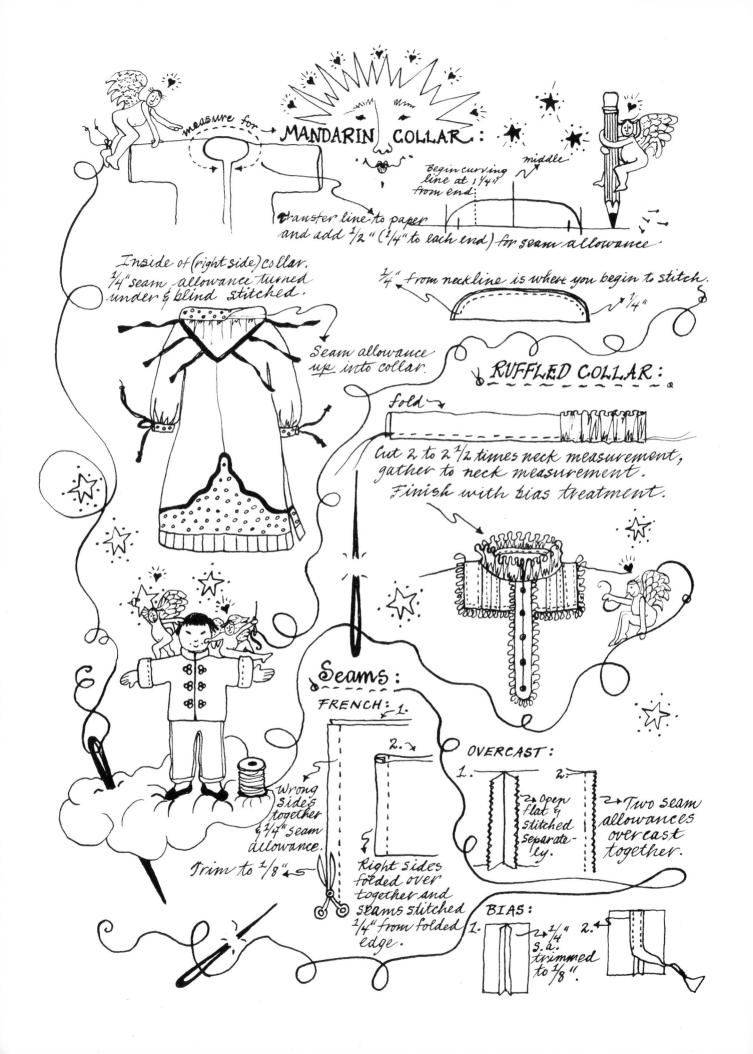

measure for → MANDARIN COLLAR:

Begin curving line at 1/4" from end. middle

transfer line to paper and add 1/2" (1/4" to each end) for seam allowance

Inside of (right side) collar. 1/4" seam allowance turned under & blind stitched.

1/4" from neckline is where you begin to stitch.

1/4"

Seam allowance up into collar.

RUFFLED COLLAR:

fold

Cut 2 to 2 1/2 times neck measurement, gather to neck measurement. Finish with bias treatment.

Seams:

FRENCH: 1.

2.

Wrong sides together 1/4" seam allowance. Trim to 1/8"

Right sides folded over together and seams stitched 1/4" from folded edge.

OVERCAST:

1.   2.

Open flat & stitched separately.

Two seam allowances overcast together.

BIAS:

1.   1/4" s.a. trimmed to 1/8"   2.

and pull the thread until you have a loop just large enough to hold in your left hand (if you sew with your right). Put that hand through the loop, catch the thread attached to the needle, and pull it through the loop. The loop will slide down to form a knot at the collar edge, and you'll now be holding a new loop in your left hand. Continue working this chain of knots until the chain is long enough to form a small loop along the collar's edge. Secure the chain to the collar with another small knot and begin another chain.

MOCK SMOCKING

Traditional smocking gathers fullness in a decorative way and at the same time gives a certain amount of elasticity to areas needing that feature. It is particularly useful at necklines and sleeves. Mock smocking takes much license with the true English smocking technique. Our method may not suit the purists, but the results are charming just the same.

Set your machine with a basting stitch and run several rows of stitching approximately ½" apart. Leave long threads at the ends. Gather the lines up evenly and tie off the long threads. Pin the garment to an upholstered piece of furniture so that you can pull down on the lengthwise grain of the fabric. Tiny pleats will form.

Thread a needle with three strands of embroidery floss (more for a heavier look), knot the thread, and bring the needle through to the right side of the garment. Catch up just a tiny bit of each pleat at intervals of ¼", or as close to that as your eye can calculate. The cable stitch for mock smocking is illustrated with embroidery stitches on page 110. Don't worry if your work doesn't look absolutely perfect! This is one of the times when a primitive look is delightful. Remove the basting stitches when your smocking is completed.

If you don't do a lot of embroidery or hand sewing, perhaps you would be wise to do a sample swatch before beginning your mock smocking project. There is a flow to the up and down placement of thread with your needle, and the appearance of your stitches improves with a little practice.

After you have completed a mock smocking project you may be inclined to do some research on proper English smocking. There are many books on this popular needle art which teach an enormous variety of smocking stitches in the pleat or dot-to-dot method. Try those methods on one of the garment patterns in this book.

107

EMBROIDERY STITCHES

The illustrations on page 110 show how to work all the stitches specified in the project instructions, and should give you lots of other design ideas besides. If you want to learn additional embroidery stitches and techniques, there are dozens of excellent books to which you can refer.

DECORATIVE TIES

Bias tape

Folded in half and sewn together lengthwise, bias tape becomes one of the easiest ties you can make for sleeve, leg, and hem casings. After the ties have been threaded into the casings, tie off the ends into knots. This gives a finished look to the raw end and eliminates the need to turn it under when sewing the bias closed. It also makes the ties less likely to disappear into the casing.

Braided yarn ties

These are fun to do, take only a little yarn or embroidery floss, and allow you to use several different colors together.

Determine the length you want your ties to be, and add an inch or so extra for knotting. Cut three strands, or groups of strands, of yarn or floss for each tie. Make an overhand knot at one end of a group of strands to fasten them together, and safety-pin securely to an upholstered piece of furniture. Braid the strands, pulling down on the yarns and pulling them tight as you work. Knot the end.

Braided yarns also make interesting applied decorations on garments. Try braiding a long piece to edge the neckline, sleeves, and front opening of a jacket or sweater or to use on a soft wool or knit dress. There are an infinite number of possibilities. Merely spot-pin the braid as you place it in your design, then blindstitch or couch it to the garment.

Hem Stitches:

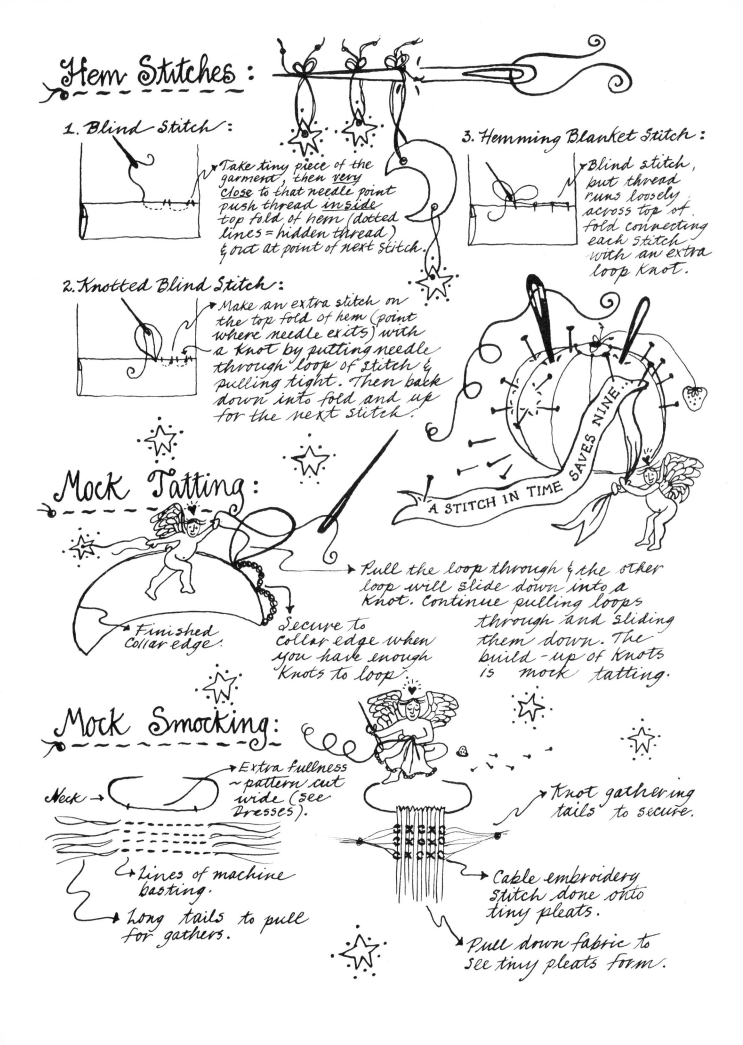

1. Blind Stitch:

Take tiny piece of the garment, then _very_ _close_ to that needle point push thread _inside_ top fold of hem (dotted lines = hidden thread) & out at point of next stitch.

2. Knotted Blind Stitch:

Make an extra stitch on the top fold of hem (point where needle exits) with a knot by putting needle through loop of stitch & pulling tight. Then back down into fold and up for the next stitch.

3. Hemming Blanket Stitch:

Blind stitch, but thread runs loosely across top of fold connecting each stitch with an extra loop knot.

A STITCH IN TIME SAVES NINE

Mock Tatting:

Finished Collar edge.

Secure to collar edge when you have enough knots to loop.

Pull the loop through & the other loop will slide down into a knot. Continue pulling loops through and sliding them down. The build-up of knots is mock tatting.

Mock Smocking:

Neck →

Extra fullness ~ pattern cut wide (see Dresses).

Lines of machine basting.

Long tails to pull for gathers.

Knot gathering tails to secure.

Cable embroidery stitch done onto tiny pleats.

Pull down fabric to see tiny pleats form.

Scandinavian twisted ties

Here's a great experience if you've never made them before! They look complicated yet are the quickest, simplest thing to do! Use single or multiple strands of yarn, crochet cotton, or embroidery floss, in a single color or several colors. Measure 2½ times the finished length for each tie, cut the yarn, and knot one end. The thickness of your finished ties will be at least double the thickness you have at this point, so before you continue, try to determine how fat you want your ties to be.

Safety-pin the knotted end to an upholstered piece of furniture, stand away from the furniture until the yarns are taut, and twist them in one direction until they are very tight. Carefully fold the twisted yarns in half, still holding them taut with both hands. Doubled, the yarns automatically twist wildly around each other. Hold onto the knotted end and smooth out the tie as it does its twisting. Knot both ends.

TASSELS

Cut a piece of cardboard the length you want the tassel. Wind one color or a variety of colors of yarn around the cardboard until you have a thickness which pleases you. Thread a needle with the main color yarn and push it through one end of the yarn. Slip the cardboard out, push the needle through one more time and knot securely. Cut the yarn. Wind the same color of yarn several times around the tassel ¼" or so from the top, and knot. Cut the ends off the same length as the tassel. Cut through the bottom loops of yarn and sew the tassel to your garment.

POM-POMS

Cut two doughnut-shaped templates of cardboard the diameter you wish your pom-pom to be. Make the center hole of the "doughnut" large enough to push a small ball of yarn through. Place the templates on top of one another and treat them as one. Holding one end of the yarn, wind the yarn around the outside and through the center of the template until the cardboard is completely covered. The thickness of the completed pom-pom depends upon how much yarn you wind around the template. When you have achieved the desired thickness, cut the yarn and then put the scissors between the two doughnuts and carefully cut the yarn around the outside edge. Guide a length of yarn between the two sections of yarn, pull tight, and knot. Remove the cardboard. Holding the piece of yarn which secures your pom-pom, strike the ball on a table to puff it out. Trim any uneven pieces of yarn.

109

MINI TASSELS AND POM-POMS

Diminutive tassels and pom-poms are available by the yard where upholstery trimmings are sold. The all-cotton varieties are still made, but may be harder to locate than those of man-made fibers. They are also sold in packets in craft stores and in some sewing and knitting stores.

If you buy them by the yard, the individual pom-poms and tassels can easily be snipped off the braid to which they are attached. (The braid can then be used as a trim.) To attach them to a garment, simply sew through the thread or wire which holds them together.

When you're thrift shopping, keep your eyes open for old trims which have tiny tassels and pom-poms woven into them. The older ones are more likely to be washable, and will probably be very affordable. There are so many ways to use these as decorations on baby clothes. They make wonderful ends for ties and for eye-catching accents on footwear. Pom-poms sewn randomly on purchased hats and sweaters can be whatever you want them to be: snowflakes, balls, fruit, tree decorations, clown "buttons," or even stars. Tassels combined with rosettes are elegant touches for fancier wear.

The one very important thing to remember when working with mini tassels and pom-poms is to sew them on **very** securely, as you would a button or other tiny applied object, for baby's safety and your peace of mind.

ROSETTES

For an elegant old-world feminine touch, nothing has quite the appeal of rosettes. Fashioned from satin ribbon, seam tape, or seam binding, then sewn on at strategic points, rosettes give the garment a beautiful, special-occasion look. Imagine them at the center or at the corners of

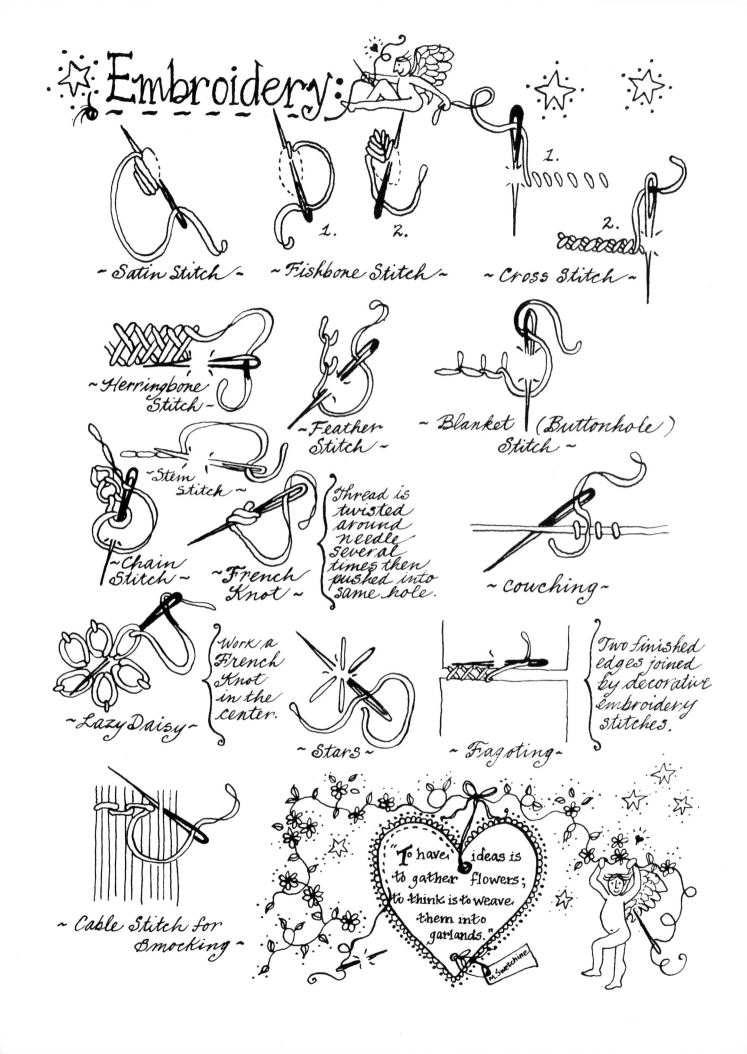

Embroidery:

~ Satin Stitch ~

~ Fishbone Stitch ~
1.   2.

~ Cross Stitch ~
1.
2.

~ Herringbone Stitch ~

~ Feather Stitch ~

~ Blanket (Buttonhole) Stitch ~

~ Stem stitch ~

~ Chain Stitch ~

~ French Knot ~

Thread is twisted around needle several times then pushed into same hole.

~ couching ~

~ Lazy Daisy ~

Work a French Knot in the center.

~ Stars ~

~ Fagoting ~

Two finished edges joined by decorative embroidery stitches.

~ Cable Stitch for Smocking ~

"To have ideas is to gather flowers; to think is to weave them into garlands."
M. Swetchine

a collar, at the shoulders with tiny ribbon streamers, at the sleeve cuffs where satin drawstrings exit, at dress yoke points, at the waist or along the hem, on the instep of a perfect pair of little slippers, or securing the ties of a lacy bonnet. Besides having all of these inspired uses, they are so easy to make!

Fold a length of ¼" satin ribbon in half lengthwise and begin coiling the folded ribbon around the raw edge. With a threaded needle, secure the bottom (selvage edges) of the coil with tiny stitches as you wind the ribbon. The folded (top) edge of the rosette will flare out slightly, and take on the appearance of flower petals. Continue until the rosette is the desired size, cut the ribbon, and fold the raw edge inside itself. Sew it closed with tiny stitches. (See illustration.) Tiny green leaves can be fashioned from satin ribbon in a similar manner, but by folding and tucking, rather than coiling, the ribbon. Experiment with different shapes. After the rosettes are sewn onto your garment you may wish to embroider small green leaves using the satin or fishbone embroidery stitches.

MOCK FROGS

As with so much of the needlework which comes from the Far East, frogs are small works of art. The meticulously twisted and sewn cording that Oriental seamstresses fashioned into kimono fasteners is still found on some contemporary garments, but antique clothing shows the frogs' beauty exceptionally well.

Many of the patterns in this book can be enhanced by frog closures, so you might keep your eyes open for special examples to accent a project. An easy alternative is to fashion your own. They are called "mock" because they are so simply made compared with the ancient ones.

The illustrated method uses single-fold bias tape, folded lengthwise then tightly coiled and blindstitched together as it is wound. Look at some of the examples and see what simple (or elaborate) "mock" frogs you can design!

KNITTING AND CROCHET STITCHES

Included here are directions for only those stitches mentioned in specific project instructions. There are many good knitting and crochet books in which you can find additional ideas and specific techniques.

111

KNITTING STITCHES

The stitches used for the knit projects in this book are not difficult ones, but if you've never done any knitting you may want to refer to a general knitting book, or have someone show you the basics, before attempting these projects.

Bobble or popcorn stitch

This is used for the sweater made from argyle socks and is also a good stitch to use as a decoration for knits you are recycling, or on purchased knits you wish to embellish with your own special touches. To work the stitch as part of a knitting project, in the stitch you wish to be a bobble:

K1, P1, K1, P1, K1 without casting the stitch off—you have 5 stitches in one. Turn. K5. Turn. P5. Turn. K5. Turn. Bind off in purl until one stitch remains. Continue knitting the row.

To apply this stitch in a line or a close pattern on top of a garment, thread a large-eyed needle with approximately a one-yard length of yarn. Choose two short knitting needles of a size to give approximately the same gauge as the garment you are embellishing, or larger if you wish to make bigger bobbles. From the wrong side of the garment insert the needle to the front and around a stitch of the garment. Then push the needle back up to the right side leaving a short "tail" on the wrong side. Pull the yarn until you have a small loop (or stitch) in which to knit your bobble. When you have cast off four of the five stitches on the bobble and have one remaining, slip the stitch off the knitting needle and put the yarn-threaded needle through that last stitch, pulling tight as you do. Push the needle to the wrong side and tie off the yarn with the tail you left at the back when you began. If you are going to make a row of bobbles, run the yarn along the wrong side of the garment to the point you wish to place another, and proceed until more yarn is needed. As you use up yarn, tie new yarn onto the old on the wrong side.

Rosettes:

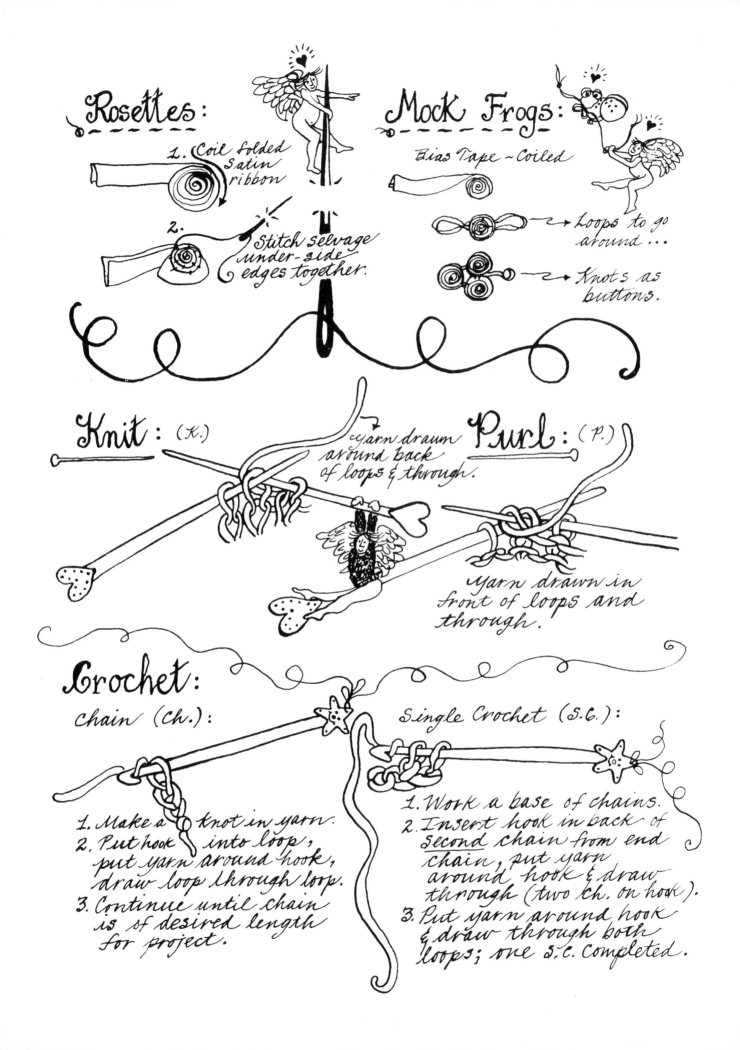

1. Coil folded Satin ribbon

2.

Stitch selvage under-side edges together.

Mock Frogs:

Bias Tape ~ Coiled

→ Loops to go around ...

→ Knots as buttons.

Knit: (K.)

yarn drawn around back of loops & through.

Purl: (P.)

yarn drawn in front of loops and through.

Crochet:

chain (Ch.):

1. Make a knot in yarn.
2. Put hook into loop, put yarn around hook, draw loop through loop.
3. Continue until chain is of desired length for project.

Single Crochet (S.C.):

1. Work a base of chains.
2. Insert hook in back of second chain from end chain, put yarn around hook & draw through (two ch. on hook).
3. Put yarn around hook & draw through both loops; one s.c. completed.

If there will be substantial space between bobbles, you may prefer to knit individual bobbles with short needles, tying them onto the sweater wherever you wish, instead of carrying yarn along the back as just described.

Seed stitch

The seed stitch is a decorative variation of the basic knit and purl stitches and has good firmness for areas where that is desired. And it is fun to use. Directions usually tell you to work it on an uneven number of stitches, but it is possible to use an even number. Just remember to begin the second, or purl, row the same as you began the first, or knit, row. As you will see from the pattern for an uneven number of stitches, if the row ends in a knit stitch, the next row begins with a knit stitch.

Cast on an uneven number of stitches. Row 1: *K1, P1; repeat from *. End with K1. Row 2: Repeat Row 1.

Checkerboard stitch

This is another combination of knit and purl stitches. It has many variations and some directions will throw in a row of knit to separate the checks, but the easy flow of K2 (or 3 or 4), P2 (or 3 or 4 —whatever you wish) on one row, the opposite on the second row, etc., is relaxing, and it's fun to watch the pattern take form.

Cast on an even number of stitches. Row 1: *K2, P2; repeat from *. Row 2: Begin with P2 if you ended K2 on Row 1. Begin with K2 if you ended P2 on Row 1. * P2, K2; repeat from *. Rows 3 and 4: Repeat Rows 1 and 2 in reverse. Rows 5 and 6: Repeat Rows 3 and 4. And so on.

CROCHET STITCHES

If this is your first attempt at crocheting, look at the illustration on page 112, and perhaps a basic crochet instruction book as well, before adding crochet to your baby garment.

Buttonhole

These buttonholes, worked in single crochet, are used on the rag strip vest (page 53) and blanket coat (page 37). Determine placement and length of buttonholes. After one row of single crochet has been run up the side of the opening which will have buttonholes, work as follows: Chain 1 (2, 3, or 4—depending on the size of the button) **over** the same number of single crochet already worked. Continue to single crochet into the row already worked. See illustration.

113

Bobble or popcorn

This decorative crochet stitch can be applied in a continuous flow connected by chain or single crochet stitch on the right side of a garment, or bobbles can be worked individually and tied on in the same manner as the knit bobbles described on page 111. The crocheted bobble is worked on a row of chains.

Chain 3. 5 DC into next (2nd) stitch. Withdraw hook from the last loop and insert it into the first of the group of 5. Pick up the dropped loop and pull through. Chain 1 into the stitch in which you originally worked the 5 chains. Continue chaining, spacing the bobbles as you desire. Or work individually and tie in a knot after the final chain stitch of the bobble, leaving long tails with which to tie the bobble onto a garment.

Karen Martin can't remember when she didn't want to "stitch a little something together." She earned her degree in applied arts from Syracuse University, and has been collecting and experimenting with textiles ever since. Karen's one-of-a-kind dolls, fashioned from collages of antique and new textiles, have won awards at museum shows in New York. She retails her clothing and doll designs from her studio, also named "Angel Threads." She lives in Westfield, New Jersey, with her husband, two children, Siamese cat, and parakeet—all perfect angels most of the time.